# COMPUTERS
## Made Really
# SIMPLE

# COMPUTERS
## Made Really
# SIMPLE

## KENT PORTER

Thomas Y. Crowell, Publishers
Established 1834
New York

Manufactured in the United States of America

Library of Congress Cataloging in Publication Data

Porter, Kent
    Computers made really simple.

    Bibliography: p.
    Includes index.
    1. Computers.   2. Electronic data processing.
I. Title.
QA76 P6525       001.6'4        75-34293
ISBN 0-690-01094-X

              83   10   9   8   7

*To Jeanne, of course*

# Contents

# COMPUTERS
## Made Really
# SIMPLE

# 1

# The Computer in Today's World

THE BIRTH of the most powerful machine in the history of the world was a singularly unspectacular event. One day late in World War II, about fifteen men filed out of a room where they had spent two and a half years building a thing called the ENIAC. They were smiling. It worked. They went home and said nothing to their wives and friends.

The ENIAC (Electronic Numerical Integrator and Computer) was the first modern computer. It was built as a secret project, financed by the government to speed up the production of numerical tables and solutions to pressing and complex mathematical problems. The world did not know of its existence. Later, when the wraps of secrecy were lifted and the scientists announced that they had created a machine that could add two numbers in 1/5,000 of a second, the world cast a distracted glance, shrugged, and went on about its business.

This was certainly no new reaction to technological revolution. When Alexander Graham Bell invented the telephone in 1872, one newspaper reflected the common view that "It is an interesting toy, useful perhaps to professors of electricity and physics, but it can never be of any practical value." Nearly everyone felt the same way about the computer. Despite the massive lack of public interest, though, there were some who saw the computer's potential, and they persevered in their laboratories and workshops. In 1951, the first commercially produced computer was delivered, and two more were installed over the next twelve months. Still the world had little understanding of what this machine was all about, and even less interest in finding out. In 1952, a man was heard on the radio describing the capabilities of the machine he supervised, and one of his comments was that it was unbeatable at tic-tac-toe. My own father had a comment that seems to summarize the overall feeling of America at that point in the computer's infancy: "It seems pretty silly to me to spend millions of dollars to build a machine to play tic-tac-toe."

The species *Homo sapiens* was unprepared for what this single invention would bring. Twenty years after the first computer was delivered, there were 80,000 of them. Knowledge, doubling in the 1940s at the rate of perhaps every twenty-five years (and this seemed dangerously fast to most people then), began doubling in exponential proportions: each time it doubled, it would take only half as long to do so again the next time. Technology split open like an overripe watermelon. New knowledge spewed forth from the computer so rapidly that it was outdated by the time it could be put to use. By the 1970s, over half the professions that occupy Man didn't even exist twenty years ago, and over half of those didn't exist five years ago.

We cannot, of course, foresee the future. In 1952, the computer was an expensive toy to play tic-tac-toe, a scientific plaything which, like the 1872 telephone, "can never be of any practical value." No one could predict that this gadget would, in the short period of twenty years, so completely change the entire society of Man that the most fanciful science fiction of those days would become the old-fashioned commonplaces of these.

Yet, whether it was foreseeable or not, the computer has become one of the indispensable frame members of the structure of society. In two short decades, the time it takes an infant to reach maturity, the entire world has become so dependent upon the computer that it could not continue to function without it.

What the computer offers us is the one thing we have never had in vast quantities: time. We have always had intelligence, imagination, intuition, ambition. But time is doled to each man in very limited amounts. (It is a tribute to the ingenuity of Man that the ancient Egyptians, with only the most rudimentary tools, built the Pyramids. However, the limitations of time are seen in the fact that these pharaohs' tombs were begun when the monarchs were born, often not yet completed when they died, and took the combined efforts of thousands to erect.) The key word in any undertaking has always been *time*. By virtue of its speed, the computer gives us this precious commodity. In *one second*, a computer can do as much arithmetic as twenty men can do in a day. By this measure, it would take over half a million people to keep pace with a single computer. Thus, in one day, a computer can give us the equivalent of 2,000 man-years of work.

This is immense power. With the computer, we have conquered the tyranny of Time. What used to take hours can now be done in millionths of a second, and tasks that could not be done at all because they took lifetimes to perform can now be accomplished in a matter of minutes.

The amount of good that can be done in the bat of an eye by the combined resources of all the computers humming at this moment would outweigh all the good that has ever been done since the first word was uttered in a cave.

But the computer is not always used to do good. The first computer, the ENIAC, was tested by working a set of problems that led to the atom bomb. Computers are used today to pry into peoples' private affairs, to replace workers who will be ruthlessly fired, to evolve plans of war, to run gangster operations. This marvelous invention is only a machine that does as it is told and makes no moral judgments about those tasks. The people who wield the power given by the computer must always be held responsible for the uses to which that power is put.

There is much controversy over the effects of the computer. To some, the very word is profanity; to others, it is the only hope. The arguments will continue as long as the computer is with us, which means that they will never end. For no matter who is right, the computer is here to stay. It touches every part of our lives. We cannot escape it so long as we remain in civilization. The computer sends us bills, receives our payments, prepares our paychecks, keeps the records of our bank accounts, diagnoses our illnesses, analyzes our voting habits. It runs factories, designs bridges, mixes cement, teaches classes, bakes bread, sends men to the Moon, predicts the weather, crushes rock, and weaves carpets.

In such a world, leaning heavily on the computer and in danger of being dominated by it, we must understand what this machine is (and is not), what it can (and cannot) do, and how it works. The importance of computers is so great that the understanding of them is necessary for anyone who must function in the world.

# 2
# What Is a Computer?

In MANY WAYS a computer is like you. You can see and hear certain things, and so can the computer. Your brain senses what you see and hear, thinks about it, and remembers it. The computer's brain does the same things. All day, every day, you compare things in your world— shall I wear this or that piece of clothing? stand or sit? am I thirsty or not?—and you make decisions about them. So does a computer. Computers, like you, can read and write. They can be told things that they will remember and use later as they do their work.

However, a computer is not a person. It is a machine which is similar in some ways to a person, but it is always (and unalterably) a machine.

Let's tag it with a definition: *A computer is a high-speed machine which performs arithmetic, makes comparisons, and remembers what it has done.* It can be told what to do and how to do it, and it can tell us the results of those instructions.

That is all a computer does. It cannot feel. It does not think as we think. It knows nothing except what we tell

5

it. If we tell it to do something the wrong way, the computer will do it the wrong way and give us the wrong answer. It has no idea of right and wrong, and it does not care. If we confuse it, it does not even try to understand. It simply gives up.

To be completely blunt (it has no feelings to be hurt), a computer is stupid. If we properly tell it what to do and how to do it, the computer is fast and accurate. Beyond this, it knows nothing.

The computer is a tool, invented by Man to make Man's work easier. It can never replace Man, because its only purpose is to help us.

## Computer Anatomy

Anatomy is the science that deals with the structure of plants and animals. It also investigates the relationships of the parts of these structures to one another. Although the computer is only a machine and not a living thing, it can be said to resemble life forms. In fact, it is more complex than some living things: bacteria, for example. We have created the computer in our own image, to act in ways that resemble our actions and to function in ways which have been proven in our own bodies. We have endowed it with organs and senses. When something is wrong with it, we diagnose it just as a doctor diagnoses a patient. So we can correctly say that a computer possesses anatomy, just as living things do. Let's look at the picture of a computer for a moment. It will show us some of the external anatomy of the machine.

Immediately we notice that the machine consists of a number of devices housed in boxes of various sorts.

These boxes are called *components*. Each component has some particular function to perform, just as each organ of the body has its own job. Not all computers use the same components, because not all computers do the same jobs. Most computers look like this one, though. This is a typical computer, of the sort this book explains.

A typical computer installation. Woman is operating the console. To her left is the Central Processing Unit. Above the console is the auxiliary storage. The page printer is at the upper right. In the background are magnetic tape drives. (*IBM Corp.*)

The components fall into four categories: *Central Processor, Storage, Input,* and *Output*. Let's talk briefly about each functional component. Later we'll discuss them in much greater detail.

1. *Central Processor* (to the left of the woman). This is the brains of the computer. If you didn't have a brain,

you wouldn't be a person. Without the Central Processor, this machine wouldn't be a computer.

2. *Storage* (within the Central Processor and directly beyond the typewriter). Storage and memory are the same in a computer. As we said earlier, the computer does three basic things: it performs arithmetic, compares, and remembers what it has done. The memory, or storage, is the part that remembers. The storage also remembers the instructions given to it by people, so that it will know what to do and how to do it. It can hold information given to it and the answers to problems already worked out.

This computer has two kinds of memory: *main storage* and *auxiliary storage*. The main storage is in the same component as the Central Processor. It is a temporary memory, holding the instructions and information for the particular job being run. The auxiliary storage beyond the typewriter in the picture holds other information on a more permanent basis. The computer can call this information into main storage as it is needed.

3. and 4. *Input* and *Output*. Consider what would happen if you were unable to speak, read, write, hear, or see. You would be cut off from the world. Even if you were smarter than Einstein, it would do you no good. You wouldn't be able to receive any information, nor could you communicate what you knew and thought to the world.

So it is with the computer. If the computer is to be of any value to us, we must be able to communicate with it. That's what input and output devices are for. You have ears, eyes, and a mouth, and you can write and manipulate with your hands. Those are your input and output devices. The computer has a different set of inputs and outputs, but they serve the same ends. They enable us to communicate our instructions and information to the computer (input) and they enable the computer to tell us what it has done with that information (output).

In the picture of the computer, different sorts of input and output components are shown. The woman is operating the computer through a set of controls called the *console,* and the computer can tell her what it's doing by typing messages on the console and by lighting lamps on the panel over her shoulder. Off to the right in the background is a *page printer,* where the computer prints the answers to problems. At the rear is a row of combined input-output devices which read and write on *magnetic tape* in a way similar to a tape recorder. The purpose of all these components is to provide communications between Man and his "mind machine."

## Data Processing System

The operation of a computer is called data processing, which is taking information in a raw form, analyzing and operating on it in order to find something out.

Suppose we are asked to find out how many station wagons and sedans are owned by the members of a social organization. First we must ask each member to indicate on a form whether or not he or she owns a station wagon, a sedan, or both. These forms will be our *data.*

Next we have to go through the forms and count the number of station wagons and sedans. This is the *processing.* The answer, when we are finished, will be the *results.*

This is a form of data processing. It is a series of

planned activities and operations on information that yields a desired result.

The term data processing system usually refers to problems like the example, but involving a computer. A data processing system includes both the computer equipment and the procedures for using the computer. In the case of our example, let's say a computer was used to count the number of sedans and station wagons. The procedures would be (1) the gathering of the data on all the cars owned by club members, (2) instructing the computer in what to do with the data, (3) feeding the data into the computer in such a way that the computer understands it, (4) actually operating the computer as it works on the problem, and (5) returning the results to whomever requested the information.

## Living Conditions

You, as a human, require certain conditions in your environment in order to live. The temperature has to be within certain limits. There must be enough oxygen present to keep your bodily functions going. You require water to drink, food to eat, and protection from "the elements."

Computers have such needs, too. A computer is very sensitive to its environment. The air must be of a constant seventy degrees and contain a low amount of humidity. Because computers are electrical machines, they create heat which must be carried off, and certain components also need special coolers. A constant flow of electricity is necessary, since the computer is an electrical machine. Computers can't stand dust and dirt. They have even been known to malfunction because of sensitivity to perfumes and after-shave lotions worn by workers.

To provide the proper environment for good computer operation, special rooms are built to house the equipment. These are called (believe it or not) *computer rooms*. Usually computer rooms are sparsely furnished places, containing only the components and other equipment needed to make the machine work. Often the floors are made of removable squares two feet on a side which rest on a framework. These squares can be lifted out to give access to the space underneath. The space is used to run the multitude of electrical cables that go among the components. In addition, cold air to cool the components is pumped through this space.

Computer rooms serve another purpose, too. They contain the noise computers make. Computers are extremely noisy machines. In truth, the computer itself is soundless, but the components have loud fans inside to keep the air in motion and carry off the heat produced by electricity. Printers, like the one at the right upper corner of the picture, make a high-pitched squeal mixed with a rapid clicking. Card readers sound like a machine gun. The operator's console rattles loudly as it types messages to the operator. So the computer room protects the machinery inside from conditions that affect it, and the people outside from the noise.

## Under the Lid

The computer is an electronic device. Electricity, as you no doubt know, is a form of energy that lights lamps and runs motors and heats stove burners and so forth.

Electronics is a different matter. Many people use the word without really knowing what it means. For purposes of clarity, we'll define it: *electronics* is the use of electricity to carry information.

Central Processor opened to show racks of circuit boards. Technician is holding one of the boards. (*Honeywell*)

Under the lids of computer components are millions of electrical devices used in the electronics of the system. These devices are called *circuits*. Electricity always flows in a circle—from a source through some resistance and back to the source. The resistance is created by the harnessing of the electricity to do some job. Because of this circular flow, the path established for it is called a circuit. Computer circuits are usually laid on thin boards of plastic which plug into racks. Each board may contain thousands of complex circuits, some of them much smaller than a speck of dust. Hundreds of these boards rest in each rack.

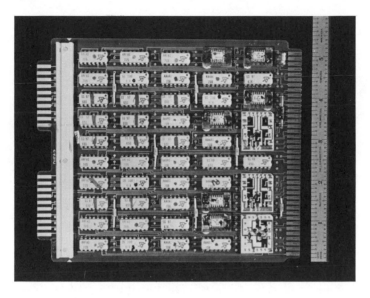

Computer circuit board. This one contains forty-seven individual circuits. Note the ruler indicating its true size. (*Honeywell*)

Every electronic circuit in the computer has some special purpose. Some add, some count, others contain instructions or remember numbers. The control section of the Central Processor knows what each circuit does and where it is.

Look at the picture of the computer room again. That woman is the most important element in the picture. Without her, the computer would be a helpless piece of junk. Without people, the computer would have no reason at all to exist.

# 3

# Computer Talk

IN THE LAST CHAPTER we said that the computer is an electronic device, and that electronics is the use of electricity to convey information.

We people, of course, convey information. This book is conveying information to you right now, using the tool of language. There are many languages around the world, each different from all the others. All of them have one thing in common, though. They are all composed of symbols—words—which mean something to the speakers of the language.

Computers use symbols also, and each symbol has some meaning all its own. Thus, computers, like people, have a language. Our language is communicated by speech and writing. The computer's is electronic.

How does electricity convey information?

Turn a light on. Now turn it off. You have just observed the two basic states of electricity. Either it's on or it's off. When the light bulb lit up, it told you the power was on. And now that it's dark again, it's telling you that the power is off.

14

Now suppose we have four light bulbs in a row, with a switch to control each one. Going from right to left, we'll number them, starting with one and doubling the number each time. We end up with something that looks like this:

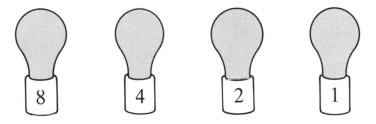

This setup will let us represent any of the sixteen numbers from 0 through 15. How?

Let's start off easy. To show a 1, we light Bulb One. All the others are still dark. The number 2 is designated by switching off Bulb One and turning on Bulb Two. I'll bet you've already figured out that to show a 4 all we do is to turn on Bulb Four while the others are dark. But wait! We missed 3. How do we show it?

Here's where the fun begins. To represent a 3, we turn on Bulbs One and Two at the same time. Anybody who can add knows that one plus two equals three. To show a 5, we light One and Four. The number 6 is Two and Four. An 11 is represented by One, Two, and Eight. In other words, to show any number up to fifteen we just turn on the bulbs whose sum will total the number we want to represent.

This scheme is called *binary numbering*. The word binary comes from a couple of Latin roots meaning "two numbers." Each light bulb has two states, on and off. Thus it can represent one of two possible numbers. If it's off, it always stands for zero. If it's on, its value is determined by its place in the row of bulbs.

Look at the row of bulbs below. Notice that Bulbs One, Two, and Four are lighted, but Eight is dark. What number is represented? What is the value of Bulb Eight?

The number shown here is 7, because $4 + 2 + 1 = 7$. The value of Bulb Eight is zero. Remember, when the bulb is off, it always means zero.

Which number is represented now?

You should have read this row of bulbs as a 15, because $8 + 4 + 2 + 1 = 15$. It's the same as the row before, except that the state of Bulb Eight has changed. Now, because of its place value, it represents an eight.

Most computers work on a binary numbering scheme like this. Through the binary scheme, four light bulbs can mean any number up to fifteen. This is electronics—the use of electricity to carry information.

*Place values* are nothing new to us. We use them in our own numbering scheme, which is called *decimal,* just as computers use place values in binary. The only real difference is that in our plan each place means some multiple of ten. In binary, each place stands for a multiple of two, since binary is based upon two possible states.

Let's talk about decimal place values for a moment. *Decimal* (the word) comes from the Latin word for "ten," which is appropriate since our numbering plan is based upon one of ten possible "states" occurring in each place. In other words, any place in a number can be occupied by any digit from 0 through 9. Take, for example, the number 324. The place value of each digit is increased tenfold each time we move to the left. The digit 4 is a unit, meaning it has a value which is some multiple of one. The digit 2 is in the tens' place, so it symbolizes not two but twenty. The 3 stands for three hundred, which obviously makes it a multiple of a hundred. If we added a fourth place, it would be worth ten times the value of the third place; in other words, a thousand or its multiple. A fifth position would have a place value of ten times the fourth's ($10 \times 1000 = 10,000$), and so on to infinity. Thus we say that our numbering plan has a *base* of ten, since each place can contain any of ten digits (0 through 9) and each place value is ten times the next lower place value.

In binary, the base is two. Remember, the light bulb can only be on or off. If we equate the dark state to the number zero and the lighted state to the number one, we can see that each place can contain one of two numbers. Since the base of numbering is two, then it follows that each position has a value of two times the next lower place. That's why the light bulbs are assigned numbers from right to left of one, two, four, and eight. If we added another bulb, it would have a value of 16 $(2 \times 8 = 16)$. Still another would be 32, the next 64, and so on.

## Binary Coding

A moment ago we supposed that the states of a light bulb could be represented by a zero for dark and a one for lighted. Computers don't look at light bulbs and read the messages in their states, but they can and do look at zeroes and ones. As with the lights, an absence of electricity is interpreted as a zero and the presence of power as a one. Likewise, each place in a string of these signals has a value to the base two (one, two, four, and eight).

These places are each occupied (or not occupied, depending upon whether it's a one or a zero) by pulses of electric power. The binary number 0101 (what's the value of this number?) is seen by the computer as blank-pulse-blank-pulse. The computer can move this 0101 (which is a five to us) from one place to another, store it, do arithmetic with it, and print it as a character 5 for people to read. So long as it remains in that order, 0101, it will always mean five to the computer. This is the basis of the whole language structure of the computer.

These electrical blanks and pulses are called *bits*. A bit is a place within a binary number which is always occupied by a no-pulse (zero) or a pulse (one) of electricity.

A *character* (such as a number or a letter of the alphabet) consists of a certain fixed number of bits. The meaning of each character is dependent upon the order of ones and zeroes. The character 0110 will always mean 6 to the computer. No other arrangements of bits will mean 6, and 0110 cannot represent anything but 6. The number of bits in a character is fixed, so that in a given computer all characters will have, say, four bits. There will never be a five-bit character, nor will there be a three-bit character or a character of any length except four bits. In this way the computer can be sure that it has all the bits before it begins to do something with a character. This is called *coding*.

A *code* is a set of characters, each consisting of a fixed number of bits, which mean something to the computer. It's like our alphabet. An R, for instance, is always an R. It is not an r, nor a J, nor a 4, just as 0110 is a single, invariable character with the unchanging meaning of 6.

## Binary Coded Decimal Numbers

As we've already seen, a four-bit character can represent any of sixteen digits. These are 0000 through 1111, or zero through fifteen. In our numbering plan to the base ten, however, there are only ten possible single-place digits, zero through nine. When a number exceeds the value nine, we have to go to a two-place number. Taking the number 11 as an example, we can see that there is a language problem between us and the computer. Eleven is a two-digit number to humans, but the single character 1011 means eleven to the computer. We don't have any single symbol to designate eleven to us as does the computer. This problem is further complicated by arithmetic. When we add 11 + 12, the total is 23, a perfectly valid number in the decimal system. When the computer adds 1011 to 1100, its symbols for 11 and 12, it finds the an-

swer 10111, meaning 23. But the character limit is four
bits, and this answer has five! The language problem is
getting steadily worse. What do we do about it?

The answer is really quite simple. Of the possible sixteen values for a four-bit character, we tell the computer
to use ten of the values and disregard the others. Each of
these ten values represents one decimal digit, so that we
arrive at a scheme like this:

| Binary character | Digital value |
|:---:|:---:|
| 0000 | 0 |
| 0001 | 1 |
| 0010 | 2 |
| 0011 | 3 |
| 0100 | 4 |
| 0101 | 5 |
| 0110 | 6 |
| 0111 | 7 |
| 1000 | 8 |
| 1001 | 9 |

Using a set of codes arranged in this way allows us to
communicate in a common language with the computer.
Our number 347 would be seen as 0011 0100 0111 by the
computer, and these characters (check the chart) corre-
spond exactly to our digits. The number 1829 is 0001
1000 0010 1001 in the computer language.

This scheme and others like it are used in most computers. The name of this plan is *Binary Coded Decimal,*
usually referred to as BCD. It is called Binary Coded
Decimal because it is a code, or set of characters, based
upon the binary numbering plan, arranged according to
the decimal system.

# 4

# Thought Processes

WE HAVE ALREADY SAID that a computer can do three basic things: arithmetic, comparing, and remembering. Now that you know the basics of computer anatomy and language, let's explore the inner workings—thought processes—of the electronic brain and see how it does these things.

## Arithmetic

Let's look at a sample problem in "human" math. It would be helpful if you'd get a piece of paper and a pencil so we can work the problem together.

Before we start computing, draw six boxes in a row and label them A through F. For this problem we'll say A = 9 and B = 3. Enter those values in the proper boxes.

You should now have something that looks like this:

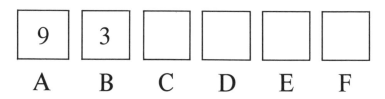

A       B       C       D       E       F

The first step is to find a value for C. If A × B = C, then we multiply the numbers in boxes A and B, entering the answer in box C.

Next let's say D = A + B. Adding the contents of A and B, we put the sum into box D.

Now we're going to subtract D's contents from the product we entered in C. The difference goes in box E, according to the equation E = C − D.

Finally, we find F by dividing what's in E by B. Our formula for this is E ÷ B = F.

Your boxes should show the following:

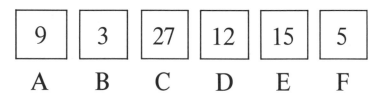

A       B       C       D       E       F

The equations to work this problem are:

A = 9
B = 3
C = A × B
D = A + B
E = C − D
F = E ÷ B

Save this paper, because we'll often refer to the problem in this chapter and several times later on in the book.

The purpose of this problem is to demonstrate how a computer does math. The boxes, the labels, and the processes are all important parts of the computer's way of doing things.

*Addition:* If you were asked to add nine to three, you would immediately answer twelve. This answer would come automatically because you have memorized tables of addition. It is merely a matter of mentally "looking up" nine plus three in your memory.

Computers don't have tables of addition memorized like you and I do. They have a faster way of adding (faster for computers, anyway). In order to find the sum of nine and three, they actually do the addition through a series of electronic circuits called, appropriately enough, *adders.*

The function of an adder is to combine two sets of binary digits to produce their sum. The adder evaluates bits of the same position in both digits according to certain rules. Since the binary code requires four bits for each numeric character, the process of adding two numbers like 3 and 9 is very similar to the method we use in decimal math for adding two four-digit numbers.

The rules for binary addition are:

$$0 + 0 = 0$$
$$0 + 1 = 1$$
$$1 + 0 = 1$$
$$1 + 1 = 0 \text{ with a 1 carried to the next higher place.}$$

To see how these rules apply, let's add the binary numbers for 2 and 3.

| *Binary* | *Decimal* |
|:---:|:---:|
| **1←carry** | |
| 0010 | 2 |
| +0011 | +3 |
| 0101 | 5 |

If you still have that paper and pencil handy, try adding the binary numbers for 3 and 6. I'll let you code them in binary and check your own answer. (A hint: Decode the answer and see if it adds up to 9.)

Now for the three and nine from the sample problem. If written out the same way, it would look like this:

| *Binary* | *Decimal* |
|:---:|:---:|
| **11** | |
| 0011 | 3 |
| +1001 | + 9 |
| 1100 | 12 |

If you decode the binary 1100, you find it equals decimal 12, which is the sum of 3 plus 9. However, it's not quite that simple. Remember, in Binary Coded Decimal we ignore any value greater than 1001 (decimal nine), so our answer is invalid. What happens now?

We turn to a procedure called *overflow*. Every computer has certain limits within which it must operate. These limits are "taught" to the computer and are a portion of the set of rules it follows. Overflow occurs whenever these limits are exceeded. An overflow always requires some action on the part of the computer. Some overflows it is taught to deal with, since they are to be expected in the course of processing. This situation is an example of a processing overflow which the computer will automatically correct. If the computer does not know how to cope with an overflow, it stops and types an overflow message to the operator.

In this case, the overflow has to do with a single-character number, twelve, which is in excess of the value limit of nine. The adder circuit has an overflow alarm which triggers a series of reactions in the computer. Basically, what happens is that binary 1010 (decimal ten) is subtracted from the sum and a one is carried to the tens' place.

For simplicity's sake we'll show this process using only decimal digits. If you wish, you can pretend they're binary numbers. The symbol * will be used to represent the unreal (binary 1100) character for 12.

As in any problem where numbers of more than one digit are added, we work from right to left, or from lower place value to higher.

| *Tens' place* | *Units' place* | |
|---|---|---|
| **1←carry** | | |
| 0 | 3 | |
| +0 | + 9 | |
| | * | Overflow! |
| | −10 | |
| 1 | 2 | and carry 1 |

$$12$$

These examples of addition should give you a feeling for the way bits are combined in order to do math. From here on, since you will probably never be summoned forth to work problems in BCD, we'll limit the examples to decimal digits.

*Multiplication* is really the same as addition. When we multiply 9 by 3, we are adding 9 to itself three times.

| Computation | Times added |
|:-----------:|:-----------:|
| 9           | 1           |
| + 9         | 2           |
| + 9         | 3           |
| 27          |             |

And isn't that the same as $9 \times 3 = 27$? This "times" business is just a shortcut we have come up with to save all that adding. The term *times* comes from "times added."

There is a shortcut method of binary multiplication similar to the one we use in decimal. (See Appendix A.) However, this system is not commonly used in computers. Electronic gadgetry is expensive. To keep costs down, the computer designers usually use "long multiplication" (multiple addition like the example above) in order to utilize the same adders for both addition and multiplication. The computer is so fast that the long way only slows it down by a few billionths of a second—scarcely worth mentioning.

To do long multiplication, a very useful device is called into service. This is the *counter,* which has scads of uses in the computer. It can be assigned to count almost anything that occurs within the machine. In this case, it counts how many times 9 is added to itself. With each addition, it increases by one and the reading is compared to the multiplier. When the counter and the multiplier are equal, the computer stops adding. The "times added" column in the example, then, is a record of counter readings at each step.

There are several ways to *subtract,* not only in the computer but in "people math" as well. The most commonly used by people is, of course, the $3 - 2 = 1$ method you learned in grade school. To us, that is the easiest and quickest way because it takes a minimum of fiddling around with the numbers and it lends itself nicely to memory tables.

To the computer, though, it is not the best way to subtract. Again, electronic circuitry is expensive and the designers are commendably aware of costs. Besides, the computer is complicated enough without cramming a lot of special subtractor circuits down its electronic throat. In order to use adders for subtraction, the designers have dredged up a little-known method called *complementing.*

At the risk of boring you with a math lesson, I'm going to walk you through an example of complementing in the decimal system. The problem is to subtract 3 from 8.

1. First we subtract 3 from 9 to find the complement. (There is an involved mathematical explanation for this, but suffice it to say here that the complement for any digit may be found by subtracting it from 9.)

2. Next we *add* 8 and the complement, 6, to get a sum of 14.

3. Now we perform a trick called *end-around carry,* which means that we cancel the 1 in 14 and add it to the 4.

4. The sum of $1 + 4$ is 5. That's the answer, and it's correct because $8 - 3 = 5$.

Written out, it looks like this:

Problem: 8 − 3
Complement of 3 = 6 (9 − 3)

$$
\begin{array}{r}
8 \\
+\ 6 \\
\hline
\cancel{1}4 \\
+1 \quad \textbf{End-around carry} \\
\hline
5
\end{array}
$$

It's apparent why complementing is not our favorite way of subtracting in decimal; we have to subtract from 9 to find the complement anyway, so we might just as well do the problem our own way and save the trouble.

Complementing, however, is easier in the computer. I promised not to blind you with any more 1's and 0's, but for a moment I'm going to break that solemn oath. To complement a BCD digit, you just change all the 0's to 1's and vice versa. To complement 3, then, we change 0011 to 1100. (It doesn't matter that 1100 is not equal to 6, the decimal complement we used above. That is a nines' complement, and this is a binary complement.) What happens from here on is the same as we did before:

Problem: 1000 − 0011   (8 − 3)
Complement of 0011 = 1100

$$
\begin{array}{r}
1000 \\
+\ 1100 \\
\hline
\cancel{1}0100 \\
+1 \quad \textbf{End-around carry} \\
\hline
0101 \quad (5)
\end{array}
$$

You may have noticed that we broke two rules about BCD digits to work this problem. The first is that 1100 has a value of 12, which is outside the range of BCD. The second is that we created a five-bit character, 10100. Don't let them bother you. These are logical characters created during the computational process. Something is always done to them after they are created, so they never leave the arithmetic unit. Any operation on such characters will always result in a real number. Case in point: 10100 was created for the purpose of being reworked by end-around carry into a real-number answer.

Just as multiplication is a child of addition, *division* comes from subtraction. Pretend that complementing is being done (which it would be in a real computer) and we'll show you how subtraction does the division portion of the sample problem:

Problem: $F = E \div B$
Values: $B = 3$ and $E = 15$

| *Computation* | *Times subtracted* |
|:---:|:---:|
| 15 | |
| $- \underline{\phantom{0}3}$ | 1 |
| 12 | |
| $- \underline{\phantom{0}3}$ | 2 |
| 9 | |
| $- \underline{\phantom{0}3}$ | 3 |
| 6 | |
| $- \underline{\phantom{0}3}$ | 4 |
| 3 | |
| $- \underline{\phantom{0}3}$ | 5 |
| 0 | |

As you can see, division is done by repeatedly subtracting the divisor (3) from the dividend (15), and count-

ing the number of subtractions it takes to reach zero. This
is another job for the counter, which in this case tells us
the answer.

Since complementing plays a part in division just as in
subtraction, the adders are used here, too. By this kind of
cleverness, all computer math is reduced to some form of
addition, so that one set of electronic adders can do any
problem.

These are the basics of computer math. The idea here
has been to give you an understanding of how the computer goes about its job, not to make you into a binary
expert. However, you may want to do something to
sharpen your skills in binary. It's fun to play with a system which is so beautifully logical. Personally, I have
found that a familiarity with binary logic greatly increases the understanding of all mathematics. (If you
share my appetite for such things, you'll find some exercises and their answers in Appendix A in the back of this
book.)

## Memory

Several times we have said that memory is one of the
key features of the computer. Most desktop adding machines can do simple arithmetic. What makes the computer unique is its ability to remember.

Basically the computer remembers two kinds of things:
what it has done and what it must do. The what-it-must-
do things are instructions written in a format known as a
*program* (to be discussed in a later chapter). For the time
being, let's limit our attention to "what it has done."

In the sample problem, we drew six boxes and labeled them A through F. These boxes constituted our "memory" for working the problem. In each box we stored some element of the problem—the original numbers 9 and 3, their sum, their product, etc.—with one box per element and one element per box. A certain set of things had to be done in order to get into a box. For instance, $E = C - D$. The only number that could possibly be entered into box E is the difference between the contents of C and D.

We labeled those boxes for a very good reason: to give them *addresses,* so that we would know where to put answers to the steps and where to look for those answers later when we needed them. An example of this is box C. We multiplied A and B to find C. Then we went on to do other things which had nothing to do with C. Later, though, we needed what was in C in order to find a value for E. The label C, or the *address,* told us where to look.

That's the way computer memories work. Within the storage sections of the computer are thousands and sometimes millions of electronic "boxes." Each box holds a certain number of bits and has a specific address. The addressing plan is obviously more complicated than single letters like F, but the principle is the same. It is the name of a distinct place, so the computer knows where to store information and where to look for it.

## Comparison

The other feature that distinguishes computers from calculators is the ability to make comparisons and act as a result of the finding. This is called *decision making.* In many ways decision making is one of the computer's most important functions. The decision is the point where a computer comes closest to human thought.

To illustrate this, let's suppose you are gift shopping for a friend. Your friend, you have learned, would like to have a stapler. You have five dollars to spend on the gift. The objective, then, is to find the best stapler you can for five dollars or less.

The first store you visit has many different staplers—electric ones, gold-plated ones, jeweled staplers, even one with a built-in combination fingernail file and spark plug wrench—but none you can afford. Thus there are many you would buy, but none you can. Decision: Look elsewhere.

The next store you go to has a lot of staplers which are much like those in the first store. However, they do have one stapler that costs less than five dollars, but unfortunately it's not a very nice one. Still, you *can* afford it. There is one more store that sells staplers. Decision: Keep this one in mind, but see what the other place has to offer.

The last store, like the one before, has a wide assortment of artful staplers and one within your price limit. You study this cheap stapler, comparing it with the other bargain. This one has rubber feet and it's easily loaded, making it a better stapler. Decision: Buy this one.

It seems likely that you don't go shopping every day for staplers costing under five dollars. You do, however, go through a hunt-and-pick process like this many times each day, making comparisons, deciding upon a course of action, and taking it.

But let's suppose that you *do* buy staplers each day as gifts for your friends. Soon you're going to get awfully

**Shopping for a Stapler**

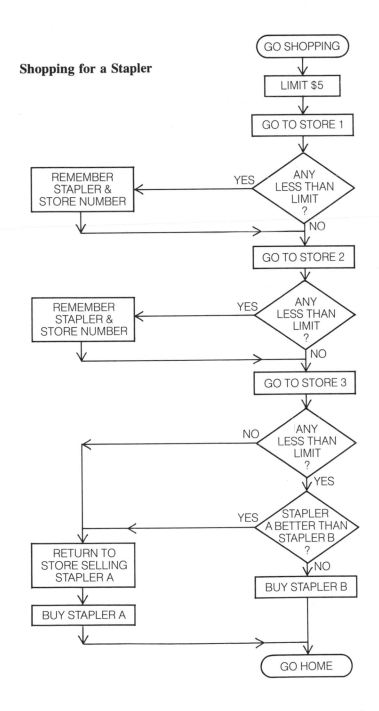

bored with touring the stapler shops. As it happens, you have a computer in a spare closet at home, so you decide to use it to do the shopping for you.

Now obviously a computer can't run around town asking questions and examining staplers. There is, however, an easy solution. *You* go to all the shops, where you collect data on every stapler: its characteristics, cost, and where it's being offered for sale. You feed all this data into your computer along with a program telling it what it has to do: find the best stapler for less than a certain amount (some friends may merit a stapler for $10, and others for only $1.29).

Just to make sure that your data processing system is in order, you test it using the same limit you had when you actually went: five dollars. Drawn pictorially, the computer's thought processes resemble the diagram. Each diamond is a decision with the two alternatives shown. The dark line shows the path actually taken.

This kind of diagram showing steps and actions to be taken is called a *flowchart*. It is widely used in creating programs for computers because it reduces a complex narrative to an easily understood picture.

There will be more on flowcharts in a later chapter. For now, its use simply illustrates the decision-making capability of the computer. This ability, as we said, is very important to us as users of the computer tool. It enables us to harness the computer and make it perform complicated tasks in which many conditions influence the answer.

Take, for instance, a computerized airline reservations system handling the needs of a person who wants to fly from Fingerstall to Wimple. A few of the many decisions the computer has to make are:

1. Does Fingerstall have airline service?
2. Does Wimple?
3. If both do, is there a direct flight between the two?
4. If not, are there other routes where connections can be made?
5. Which of the other routes is most convenient?
6. Is there a seat available on every part of the trip?
7. If not, which way is second best?
8. Are there seats available that way?
9. How much is the fare?

Were it not for the computer's ability to make decisions and then take fast action based upon the decisions, people would still be figuring out such complex problems by old time-consuming methods. But the computer does decide, and it does it a whole lot more quickly than we do.

In numeric comparisons, there are three possible results: less than, greater than, and equal to. Let's compare two numbers which we'll call M and Q, using the standard mathematical symbol $>$ to mean greater than and $<$ to mean less than. We find that $M < Q$ if $M = 4$ and $Q = 6$; that $M = Q$ if both equal 11; and that $M > Q$ when $M = 9$ and $Q = 3$.

Computers are much more exact than people. For example, if a computer compares two numbers, .000039 and .000038, it regards the first as absolutely greater than the second. In most cases we people wouldn't bother with such a tiny difference.

But to a computer, a comparison invariably means a decision, and a decision always dictates the course of subsequent action. For example, if $M < Q$, print the answer; if $M = Q$, read another card; if $M > Q$, stop execution of the program. Computers are imbeciles, and imbeciles cannot judge "just about" or "close enough"; they must be precise.

When we sent the computer shopping for a stapler, we told it the price limit was $5. What the computer did was to compare the price of every stapler to that limit. Those below the limit it remembered. Those above, it ignored. When it had separated the cheap staplers, it compared their qualities and made the choice. Had it found a solid silver stapler studded with diamonds for $5.01, it would have ignored it despite the bargain it was, because $5.01 is more than $5.00. The computer does exactly as it is told, and not a penny's worth more.

# 5
# More about Language

Up to this point, we have limited the computer's language to numbers. In the BCD system presented in Chapter 3, we found that a four-bit code structure will provide us with sixteen possible characters from 0000 to 1111. This severely restricts the computer. In our alphabet we have twenty-six letters, ten digits, and a whole bucketful of other symbols. In the alphabet we've given the computer there are only sixteen possible characters, of which ten are already committed to numerals. Yet anyone who has ever received a magazine in the mail, a bill from a major company, or a report card from a large school knows that computers print letters.

This is made possible by the *extension* of codes. There are almost as many extended coding schemes as there are models of computers. The code structure we're going to focus on is one of the most popular because it is used in one of the most common computer models, the IBM System/360. As an added benefit, it is also a logical extension of the Binary Coded Decimal system we already know about. The language's name is the Extended Binary

Coded Decimal Interchange Code. You must admit that that is a very awkward, hard-to-manage set of words, no matter how descriptive they may be. For this reason, they have been abbreviated to the slightly less jawbreaking abbreviation EBCDIC. The abbreviation has enormous appeal to computer people, who enjoy cloaking their profession in the mysteries of unfamiliar and terrifying terminology. Yet even they find EBCDIC difficult to say without getting a cramp in their tongues, so they pronounce it Eb-suh-dick, or sometimes EE-be-dick.

Now to the logic of EBCDIC. A four-bit code, as we well know, has the sixteen possible bit patterns 0000, 0001, 0010 . . . 1111. With it we have to represent 26 letters (52 if we want both upper and lower case), 10 digits, perhaps 20 punctuation marks of various sorts, and some special symbols for math use such as exponents and the operands (division, plus, minus, equals, etc). There are probably about a hundred characters in all. Then looking inside the computer, we find uses for a lot of additional characters to control functions of components, start and stop operations of various sorts, bracket certain types of data for special handling, and do a whole raft of other jobs. Let's say another 50 characters, so we need a minimum of 150 bit patterns to represent them.

By extending the binary code sequence according to the rule of two times the previous place value, we find that a seven-bit character has 128 combinations (64, 32, 16, 8, 4, 2, and 1 all added together come to 127, plus one for the zero equals 128), which are not enough to fill the need. Adding an eighth place with a value of 128, we now have 256 possible bit patterns, which leaves plenty of room for growth beyond the required 150.

This sounds pretty good until we realize that we really

haven't accomplished a thing. Remember, we told the computer to ignore any binary number greater than 1001. In an eight-bit scheme, we have to tell it that there is no valid number greater than 00001001. That means that now, instead of disregarding a mere six characters, the computer has to ignore 246. In other words, it's not going to pay any attention to any of the characters we gained by expanding the code.

The EBCDIC code has the answer for this problem. It uses an eight-bit structure, all right, but instead of a character consisting of eight continuous bits in a stream from place values 1 through 128, it is broken into two four-bit characters. The first four bits are a *classification character*. The other four are the character itself. Thus we have sixteen classifications of sixteen characters each. This achieves 256 characters, just as eight continuous bits do. The difference is in how the computer looks at each character.

For example, all numeric characters are the same as in our old friend BCD, except that now they are preceded by the classification character 1111. When the computer sees 1111, it knows that the next four bits are a number. If it is going to perform a math operation with the number, let's say putting it into an adder, it simply puts the 1111 aside. This is rather like receiving a letter in the mail. The envelope tells you that this is a letter. It delivered the contents to you and enabled you to recognize it as a letter, but once you have it the envelope is no longer of use. You take out the letter and discard the envelope. In a similar way, the computer reads the *information character* (last four bits) and puts aside the classification character.

The other classifications work in much the same way;

binary 1100, 1101, and 1110 signal the capital-letter classifications, with the next four bits specifying which letter. The character 1100 0001 means A, and 1101 0001 is J. 1000, 1001, and 1010 classify lower-case alphabetics. 0100 through 0111 signify special characters such as $, &, +, and so forth. The remaining bit patterns, 0000 through 0011, are used for internal control by the computer. They are the messages sent through the system's nerves in order to control its muscles.

The EBCDIC code has many bit patterns that are not assigned. These are scattered throughout the classifications. At the present time not all 256 bit patterns are needed. The unassigned patterns are available as new characters are required.

These bit patterns are not truly characters because they consist of two distinct elements—classifier and information. Therefore, to identify them as a particular kind of character, they have been given the name "bytes," (pronounced "bites").

The term byte is widely used in the data processing business. The capacity of a memory system, for instance, is usually measured in bytes. We might say that a particular computer has a 256K memory. This means the memory holds 256,000 bytes.

# 6

# The Brains
# of the Computer

THE MOST IMPORTANT PART of your body is your brain. Everything that makes you a human is centered there. Your brain controls your body, of course, just as the brain of any creature controls it. Its prime function is to coordinate the activities of the muscles and organs. But in addition to that, the human brain contains your intelligence, memories, and personality. It learns and then directs you as a response to the learning.

For example, it has learned to interpret symbols on paper as information, and now you are reading this book. From it you are learning more, and at the same time certain brain-controlled bodily functions such as the movement of eyes and the turning of pages are being performed. When you have finished this book, you will know something about computers, but you will probably want to know more. If so, your brain will direct you to seek other books and sources of information. If not, your brain will not spur you on to further action, and that too can be regarded as a result of learning, since you will know enough to be satisfied. If you had no intelligence,

41

you wouldn't be reading this book at all, nor would you read any other book. For without intelligence, there would be nothing about you except your shape to distinguish you from any other animal.

Religion teaches us that God made Man in his own image. Obviously we men are something less than God. By this same line of reasoning, Man has made the computer in his own image, and it is something less than us. There is nothing wrong in this; in fact, it's as it should be. We, perhaps, are a tool of God. The computer is indisputably a tool of ours. It is built to make up for some of our shortcomings. There is an old saying about the relationship between men and computers:

> Man is slow, sloppy, and incredibly brilliant;
> The computer is fast, accurate, and incredibly stupid.

A Central Processing Unit. The cabinets are about the same height as kitchen counters. (*Honeywell*)

We and our computer complement each other. Since 1951, when commercially produced computers began to fill the gap in our abilities, we have more than doubled our knowledge twice. This means that within the memory of most people now living, we have learned over twice as much as we learned in all the millions of years since the first ape decided to move into a cave. The computer has made this possible.

The computer, as we said, was made in our image. Since the largest piece of our image has to do with our brain, the largest part of the computer is *its* brain. The computer's brain is called the *Central Processing Unit.*

## Physical Aspects

Turn back to the picture of the computer in Chapter 2. In the foreground is the Central Processing Unit (CPU), just beyond the operator. In appearance the CPU is a large and rather unexciting metal box. Its face is a panel containing various lamps and switches, which enable it and the operator to communicate. Attached to it is a type-writer. The CPU types messages to the operator on this console printer, and the operator can type instructions to the CPU. The exchange of messages and instructions concerns the programs the computer is running and the way it's running them.

The CPU is like the human head. All parts of the computer system look to it for direction and fall under its control. All "thought" occurs in the CPU, and the components respond to the results of the thoughts.

The CPU is an electronic device, and it generates a lot

of heat as it works. Thus it must be cooled. In older computers air conditioners are used, and noisy fans blow cool air among the inner workings. In some newer computers, especially the giant machines, cooling is accomplished by a network of pipes carrying very cold water. Since heat is picked up by cold, the water flowing through the CPU plumbing absorbs the heat from the electronics and moves it out.

Inside the CPU are many different things: a framework of steel, miles of wire to move data and electrical energy from place to place, power supplies, memory banks, switches, circuit boards, and a multitude of other devices. The computer is built to do a complex job, and this makes it a complex machine.

In size, the CPU is shrinking as time passes and newer machines replace older models. Yet these new smaller CPU's can do much more work much faster than their larger ancestors. The reason for this goes beyond considerations of floor space and the cost of sheet metal. Electricity moves at a speed of about 186,300 miles per second. In a machine in which operations are timed in billionths of a second, the distance signals have to travel influences the machine's speed. The shorter the wires, the faster the machine.

As a by-product of this trend toward smaller machines and shorter distances, lower costs have been realized. When the transistor replaced the vacuum tube, it was found that costs fell because transistors do not require glass housings, fancy sockets, and involved filaments. Now new techniques have come along, and a chip containing thousands of transistors can be made from a single metal piece the size of one old transistor. As an example of how tiny these "solid-state" devices are, a single speck of dust will cover three or four transistors. We are close to the day when the electronics of an entire television set will be contained on a chip smaller then a postage stamp. The result of this miniaturization (making things ever smaller) has been a continual lowering of computer costs in terms of their capabilities. The latest computers work thousands and even millions of times faster than early computers, yet costs have not increased significantly.

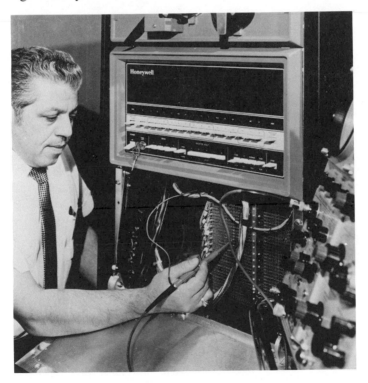

Inside a small computer. The technician is checking circuits. (*Honeywell*)

Make no mistake, though. Computers are very, very expensive. A small computer will cost at least $50,000, and the larger machines run into the millions. Much of the money is here in the CPU. The "size" of the CPU, which actually refers to its speed and not to the dimensions of its housing, is what determines the capabilities of the data processing system. The "bigger" the CPU, the more it costs and the more it can do.

## CPU Components

The CPU has two main functional areas. These are the *control unit* and the *arithmetic/logic unit*. Both are normally housed in the same box, and they work so closely together that neither can perform without the other. The two, in turn, are wholly dependent upon the *main storage* (discussed in the next chapter). Together, the three units—control, logic, and memory—comprise the brains of the computer system.

1. *Control Unit.* Within your brain is a certain area which is responsible for the coordination of your body. It takes signals coming to it from various parts of your mechanism, interprets them, and takes action upon them. For example, if you touch a hot iron with your fingertip, a signal travels to your brain's control section through a nerve, is interpreted as pain, and causes the control center to send back orders to your muscles to jerk the fingertip away. The control section also translates your thoughts into actions. If you want to cross the room, you decide to cross the room and then you give that decision to your control unit. It takes command and coordinates

the complex series of muscular activities that takes you where you want to go. This control unit also keeps house in your brain. It knows where to look for the memory of what you got for Christmas last year, and tells your brain where to store the information you're getting from this sentence. It is, in effect, the boss of your brain.

The computer's control unit does the same jobs for it. It controls every part of the machinery. The program of instructions and commands from the operator are understood by the control unit and translated into action. The control unit moves data about within and among the components, turns devices on and off, and directs the arithmetic/logic unit.

To see how the control unit operates, let's go through one of the equations in the sample problem at the beginning of Chapter 4. Memory location A contains the number 9, and B is holding a 3. The control unit receives the instruction $D = A + B$. Here's what happens:

a. The command is interpreted as meaning "add the contents of locations A and B and store the answer in D."

b. The control unit directs the arithmetic/logic unit to prepare for addition, and designates an adder circuit to do the job.

c. It tells the memory to send the contents of location A into the arithmetic/logic unit.

d. Next it tells the memory to send the number from B into the logic unit. These two steps, c and d, are called the *fetch cycle*.

e. With both numbers to be added now in the arithmetic/logic unit, the control unit orders the adder to go to work. This is called the *execute cycle*.

    f. When addition is finished, the control unit moves
the sum out of the logic unit and tells the memory to store it in location D.

    2. *Arithmetic/logic unit.* As the name indicates, this
unit is the area in which arithmetic and other logical
operations are performed. Arithmetic operations, of
course, involve adding, dividing, subtracting, and so
forth, plus more complicated functions such as rounding,
finding square roots, and changing signs. The most common *logical operation* is that of examining and discern-
ing relationships, or comparing. The work of the arithme-
tic/logic unit is done by a group of devices known as
*logic circuits.* These are electronic devices which perform according to certain preset rules.

    The basic component of the logic unit is the *accumula-
tor.* This is a temporary memory that accepts numbers or
letters sent to the logic unit from main storage. It also
holds answers produced by the adders. This makes the
accumulator rather like a doorway linking the logic unit
with the rest of the world. Both inward and outward traffic passes through the accumulator. It also stores partial
answers during computation. While the accumulator is
the focal point of the logic unit, it does very little more
than act as a waiting room.

    Another of the basic logic circuits is the *half adder.*
This circuit looks at two bits, the same place value from
each of two numbers, arriving at the same time. One bit
comes from the accumulator, the other from main memory. If both bits are blanks, or zeroes, its output is a zero.
If either bit is a pulse, or one, and the other a zero, the
half adder emits a 1 on the output side. If both are 1's,
the output is a zero and a second output wire carries a

one. This second output is the carry to the next higher place. In this way, the rules of binary addition are satisfied by electronic means.

### Half adder behavior

| Inputs | Output |
|--------|--------|
| 0 + 0  | 0 |
| 0 + 1  | 1 |
| 1 + 0  | 1 |
| 1 + 1  | 0 and a carry of 1 |

This set of behavior patterns, as you see, is the same as the rules of binary addition.

An adder is a number of half adders arranged so that carries are made from lower-order to higher-order place values. This is the workhorse of the computer, as you saw in the chapter on math.

How do all these pieces fit together to make the brains work? Let's take an example where we add two numbers, 24 and 43. These numbers are stored in memory addresses M and X. If the equation is $J = M + X$, the sum is to be stored in location J. The sequence is as follows:

a. The control unit interprets the command.
b. The control unit tells the arithmetic/logic unit to clear the accumulator of any digits remaining from previous use and set all values to zero.
c. The number found in location M (24) is fetched and moved into the accumulator.

Accumulator  | 0 | 0 | 0 | 2 | 4 |

d. The value in X (43) is moved to the adder, and at the same time the quantity in the accumulator is sent to the adder. Both numbers arrive together.

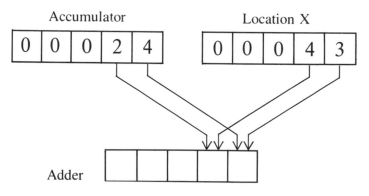

e. The control unit instructs the adder to do binary addition. The sum is stored in the accumulator, replacing the number 24 which had been there.

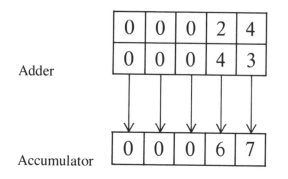

f. The control unit sends the contents of the accumulator to the memory unit with instructions to store it in address J. (Note: The accumulator still contains 00067, even though it has been read and moved to storage. For this reason, one of the first steps in any arithmetic operation is always to clear the accumulator.)

Both the arithmetic/logic unit and the control unit contain a number of temporary storage devices called *registers*. Registers are usually of a fixed length. They hold bits taken from memory that will be returned to memory. The accumulator is an example of a register. In most computers, there is a companion to the accumulator called the R-register. This register is used whenever the number of bits to be stored in the accumulator is greater than its size. For example, if the accumulator can hold only ten digits and it is necessary to store twelve, the R-register is activated. It accepts the lower-order bytes, while the two highest-order digits go to the accumulator.

The control unit uses several registers. The most important are the I-register and the S-register. The I-register retains the instruction being excuted by the control unit. The S-register contains the memory address of the next instruction. As an instruction is completed, the control unit uses the S-register reading to find the next command in memory.

Let's move a little farther into the brain now and examine the memory.

# 7

# Memory

YOU HAVE SEVERAL different kinds of memories in your brain which are used in various ways.

For example, you have a *short-term memory* that keeps track of immediate concerns. These are things like where you put your glasses when you took them off, an appointment at five o'clock today at a certain place, or who won the game last weekend. Normally these short-term memories are not terribly important and it requires little effort to recall them. They are close to the forefront of your conscious thought. After a while you erase them, as when you have your glasses perched back on your nose or after you've had your appointment.

Then there are the *long-term memories,* which you retain over extended periods and perhaps all your life. Examples of long-term memories are the name and characteristics of a childhood friend, the vacation you took in 1969, the car your father owned that never worked right, or the fistfight you had with the neighborhood bully when you were eight. These are things you store and recall with a bit of effort. They are not close to the concerns of everyday life, but occasionally you call them forth to serve some purpose. As a rule, they lay unnoticed and unused over long periods of time.

Last, but perhaps most important, you have a special type of long-term storage for *learned memories*. You remember, for instance, how to read and write. We mentioned in Chapter 4 the math tables you have committed to memory. Elderly people who haven't been on a bicycle in half a century mount up and ride away, because this is a learned skill. Learned memories are long-term tools you use automatically (and usually unconsciously) to accomplish a task. They form the basis of knowledge.

Computers have these three classifications of memory, too. Their names are different from the names we used to describe human memory systems, but the functions and uses are the same.

1. Short-term: This is the *main memory* we saw in the last chapter. Main memory contains the data and the instructions being used right now by the CPU, as well as other information requiring the attention of the processor. Main memory also has other names: processor storage, main core, main storage, and working storage.

2. Long-term: This memory stores data and programs not immediately needed by the CPU. Some programs are kept here on file all the time, while others may be fed in this morning and saved until time is available to run them this evening. Long-term memory has many names: on-line storage, mass storage, random files, and auxiliary memory are the more common terms. Sometimes it is also called by its type: drum, disk, or cell.

3. Learned: Just as your knowledge is the most important part of your memory, so is it the most important part

of the computer's. This group of memories tells the computer how to do its basic task: addition, comparison, etc. It comes as part of the computer, since the machinery would be a useless collection of junk without it. Learned memory is commonly referred to as the *executive program* or as the *software*.

Before we delve into these memory systems and learn how they operate, let's take a brief look at the organization of computer storage.

In Chapter 5, we made the discovery that characters are usually referred to as bytes, and that a byte consists of eight bits. To carry that another step, computers normally work in *words*. A word, in "computerese," is a group of so many bytes, say five or ten, which are handled as units within the computer. Word lengths vary from computer to computer. When data is moved inside the machine, for example from main storage to the logic unit, an entire word is moved. In the case of a number like 24 in a machine using five-byte words, the word would be 00024. A number like 12,345,678 would be handled as two words, 00123 45678.

Memory systems are organized according to the word length used by the computer. Each memory address will hold the number of bytes required to make a complete word. Again, referring to the sample problem in Chapter 4, each location is a box with a label called an address.

Every single memory location within the computer system has an address. In this way, the computer knows where to go to get any word it needs. The memory systems have control sections to keep track of where things are. This is like the telephone system in your town. Let us suppose that every home and business has a phone

number which is its "address." The control section is the
telephone directory. If you want to call me, you look up
my number in the directory and then dial accordingly. In
response to your command, which in this case is the output from the dial on your phone, the switching equipment
opens a path from your line to mine. Similarly, the computer's control unit "looks up" the address of the needed
information and then opens a path between that location
and another storage device such as the accumulator or a
register.

No matter what kind of memory system we refer to,
then, the organization is something like this:

| Address | Word |
|---------|-------|
| 0001 | 00009 |
| 0002 | 00003 |
| 0003 | 00027 |
| 0004 | 00012 |
| 0005 | 00015 |
| 0006 | 00005 |

## Short-Term or Main Memory

If you are going to bake a cake, you must make certain
preparations. First you examine the "program," or rec-
ipe, to find out what ingredients are needed, and you
collect them to make certain you have them all. Then you
gather the necessary tools: pots, pans, spoons, and all the
other equipment. You make certain there is adequate
space on the work counter, and you turn on the oven so it
will be ready to receive the cake. Finally, you begin.

When the control unit gets ready to run a job, it goes

through the same sort of preparations. It reads the program from input devices, or moves the instructions out of auxiliary storage, placing them in main memory. It reviews the program, making certain everything is there and that there are no unknown commands to create confusion. The necessary data is brought into main core and when enough space has been set aside to work in, the control unit clears the accumulator and begins to run the job.

Nearly all these activities involve main memory. The main memory is, along with the control and logic units, the center of the computer system. The computer can work without auxiliary storage, and during job runs it is possible to do without inputs and outputs, but unless main memory, logic, and control are singing in harmony, the computer can't run at all.

As the program is worked, the control unit moves information in and out of memory. Instructions are read from memory by the I-register of the control unit. If output is ordered by the program, it is read out of main memory. Likewise, additional inputs are read into memory during the program run if required. Messages to and from the human operator pass through main memory. In short, every movement of information in the computer system involves main memory.

How does this frantically busy system work? The most common main memory uses a network of tiny iron rings called *cores* (from which the name "main core" is derived). These cores look like doughnuts, and they are strung on a screen of wires that are finer than hairs. Each tiny core can be magnetized in either of two directions by an electrical pulse of a certain strength. If the core is magnetized in a clockwise direction it represents a binary one, and in a counterclockwise direction it means binary zero. It takes eight cores to store one byte.

When electricity passes through a wire, it sets up a magnetic field around the wire. This field is directional, so that a pulse traveling down the wire will set up a field of magnetic energy spinning in a clockwise direction with respect to the source. If you were sitting atop an electrical source wearing special glasses that enabled you to see magnetic energy, when the source sent out a pulse you would see magnetism circling the wire from left to right. The energy of this field is measurable, and it affects iron objects within its range. A certain amount of magnetism will force the iron atoms to rearrange, making the object itself a magnet. In the familiar bar magnet, there is a north and a south pole, and the magnetic energy flows from the south to the north inside the bar, then jumps outside and returns to the south end. In core magnets, the energy remains within the iron ring, constantly flowing in the direction in which the core was magnetized by the field around the wire.

It requires a certain amount of force to magnetize a core. In memory, each core is positioned at the intersection of two wires on the screen. If we want to magnetize a particular core, we find the two wires that come together inside the "doughnut hole" of that core. To each we apply half the current necessary to magnetize it. The core at the intersection of the wires feels the full energy, half from each wire, so it magnetizes.

If the current flows up and to the right in the two wires, the core magnetizes in a counterclockwise direction, signifying a binary 0. If the pulses travel down and to the left, the core's magnetic field is reversed (clockwise), meaning a binary 1. The pulse lasts only the tiniest fraction of a second, yet the core remains magnetized. It will stay magnetized in that direction forever unless another set of pulses in the opposite direction changes it. This process is called *writing in core*.

No two wires cross at more than one point. Each crossing occurs inside the hole of a core. There are many cores strung along both wires, so that every vertical wire crosses every horizontal wire and each intersection is within a core. However, as in the drawing, there is only one intersection of wires 2 and B. Thus only the core at 2B feels enough magnetic energy to be affected. All the other cores along wires 2 and B experience only half the power they need to magnetize, which is not enough to change them. In this way, by selecting two wires out of the entire grid, one core can be magnetized without affecting the others.

How does all this pulsing and magnetizing relate to the memory's function?

The cores, as we said, are arrayed on grids of crossing wires. Usually a grid, or to use its proper name, a *plane*, consists of thousands of cores. These planes are stacked vertically, one atop the other, with one plane for each bit position in the computer word. If the computer word length is five bytes, there will be forty planes in a *memory module* since five bytes times eight bits per byte equals forty bits. When a word is to be stored, the bits are read into the memory module with each bit appearing on a different plane. The bits are all stored at the same crossing, say 2B, one bit on each plane. Thus the bits are stacked straight up and down in the memory module as a word. The intersection 2B is the same for them all, with only the plane differing from bit to bit.

Intersection 2B, then, is the address of the word.

# Writing a Bit in Core Memory

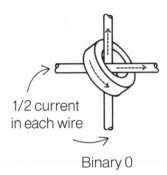

1/2 current
in each wire

Binary 0

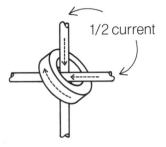

1/2 current

Binary 1

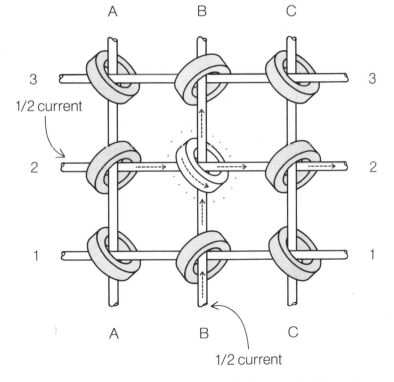

Selected Core 2B Magnetized. Others Unaffected.

## Memory Module

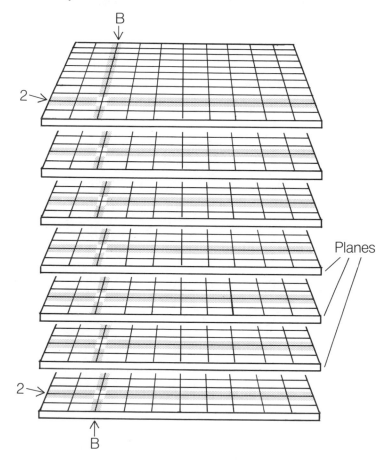

It does no good to write anything unless it can be read. How does the computer read from core? Up to now, we have spoken only of the vertical and horizontal wires on a plane which intersect within the cores. There is a third wire we have not mentioned. This wire runs diagonally through the cores at a 45-degree angle to the writing wires. Its purpose is to read from memory.

As you know, a core magnetizes in one direction or the other according to the magnetic field set up by current in the writing wires. What we didn't tell you is that if the core is remagnetized, "flipped," in the opposite direction it sends out a tiny pulse of the magnetic energy which usually remains inside the core.

Now it stands to reason that if a current in a wire will create magnetism around the wire, then the reverse also holds true. Thus a magnetic field around the wire will cause electricity to flow in the wire. This is called *induction*.

If a core is magnetized clockwise and we apply current to its crossing wires to flip it to the counterclockwise direction, it will emit a pulse of magnetic energy. All that is needed to detect the pulse is a wire in which the magnetism can induce current. This is the function of the diagonal wire.

The wire, or *sensor,* passes through every core on the plane. Only one sensor is needed on each plane, since only one address is read at a time. To read a core, the memory writes a zero on the crosswires for the address in question. If the core is magnetized to store a 1 bit, it will flip. This induces a pulse of current in the sensor for the plane. If the core is set to zero, no current will be induced, since the core does not flip. In this way, pulses and blanks (1's and 0's) are read from memory. All the planes are read at once, and each plane's sensor is monitored by the system. Without further handling, the bits can be sent as read to their new location.

The reading, however, creates a problem. If all the cores for the address are changed to zeroes in order to detect the presence of 1's, then the information that was stored there is erased. If the computer needs that information again (as it did with the 3 stored in location B in the sample problem), it will find nothing but 0's the next time it tries to read the address.

To prevent this, the memory system automatically rewrites whatever is read. The process is instantaneous, so that the word is never lost.

Although the activities of core storage may appear to be lengthy, the actual time used by the computer to read or write in core is measured in millionths or billionths of a second. Core is the fastest type of storage in common usage today.

An example of the speed of core can be seen by examining one of the latest computer models in action. This computer reads an instruction, interprets it, clears the accumulator, moves the words for two numbers to the logic unit, adds them, and returns the answer to main storage. Time: *fifty-three billionths of a second!*

Core is truly astonishing for all its complexity. It would seem perfectly reasonable to wonder why all computer memory isn't core so that everything stored in the machine would be instantly available to the CPU. The problem is that magnetic core costs many times more than other slower memories of the same size. For this reason, most computers have only as much core as they need to work efficiently. Other slower-speed storage requirements are met with auxiliary memory.

## Long-Term Memory

Auxiliary storage systems are a great deal simpler than main memory. By a strange coincidence, in memory systems the most complex, core, is the fastest, while the simplest are slowest. The main features of auxiliary memory are that it holds great masses of information and it works under the direction of the control unit.

The two most common mass storage units are the *drum* and the *disk*. They are somewhat alike, but there are a few important differences.

*Drum storage* uses a large round tube that spins on an axis at high speed. The drum is covered with a smooth brown metallic substance similar in appearance to Teflon or to the coating on a recording tape. When a magnetic field touches this material, it becomes magnetized in the area which is touched. As with core, it remains magnetized forever unless something is done to demagnetize it.

While the drum spins, its surface passes devices called *heads*. The heads are electromagnets, which only emit a magnetic field when current is passing through the wires wound around them. If a pulse of current flows through the head's windings, the resulting field causes a spot of magnetism to be written on the drum's coating. The spot represents a 1 bit. The absence of a spot is a 0.

The bits of each byte are recorded side by side on the drum's surface. The bytes of a word are arranged one above the next. A whole series of words are strung around the drum in a continuous belt. This belt is called a *channel*. The location of the channel is determined by the position of the heads that read and write on it. Each word position in the channel has an address, just as each word position in main memory has one. There is usually a set of heads for each channel, and anywhere from 50 to several hundred channels per drum.

Reading from the drum is much like writing on it. In fact, the same heads are used for both. If the head is told to read, it "watches" the surface passing under it. When a spot of magnetism passes, current is induced in the head. This sends out a pulse on the read sensor. When no magnetic spot passes, no current is induced, and thus no current flows in the sensor. This corresponds to the 1 and 0 bits respectively. Notice that reading from a drum does not erase the bits recorded there. The only way to erase bits from the drum is to write over them.

We speak of auxiliary storage as being a slow-speed memory, implying that it takes quite a while to write information on it and to read it out. This "slow speed" is slow in terms of the CPU and main memory, but not in relation to humans. For example, one computer manufacturer markets a drum unit with a capacity of over six billion bytes, and the average time needed to find and read data from it is about 1/10 of a second. In human terms, this means finding and reading one particular word in a book two million pages long in about the time it takes to blink your eyes! Remember, though, that this is a long time in a machine that measures its progress in billionths of a second. A medium-sized computer can easily do one hundred thousand operations in 1/10 of a second. Thus, drum storage is slow. Its advantage is that it can store enormous amounts of information at a relatively low cost.

*Disk storage* is similar to drum, and in fact is a direct descendant of it. Instead of a cylindrical shape, the disk is a flat plate about the size of a long-playing phonograph record. Both surfaces are coated with the same brown magnetic substance that drums wear. A typical *disk pack* consists of half a dozen of these disks mounted on the same axis with an inch or two of open space separating the surfaces.

Information is recorded on both sides of each disk in

the pack. There are channels on the surfaces arranged in concentric circles around the axis. The disk pack spins rapidly and movable heads slide back and forth under the control of the CPU to read and write on the addressed channels. Bits are recorded, as in drum storage, by tiny magnetized spots.

The capacity of a disk pack is somewhat less than that of a drum. However (and this is the big advantage of disk over drum) the packs can be easily changed, rather like changing records on a phonograph. The packs aren't ex-

Disk drives. The operator is lifting out a disk pack. One of these packs will contain 18.4 million characters. (*Honeywell*)

pensive and they take up less space than a hatbox. This enables the computer user to maintain a *library* of disk packs with each unit containing special information not always needed by the machine. For instance, in a computer center that sends bills to customers once a month, the mail addresses of the customers are only needed when the bills are run. These addresses can be stored on a disk pack. When the billing program is about to be run, the pack is mounted on a disk drive. Any changes of address are fed in and the disk files are updated. Then, during the actual billing program run, the computer reads the ad-

Data cell drive. Each cell has two vertical faces and snaps out by pulling the small handle at the top. The entire unit turns to find a card. Note the tops of the cards. They hang inside the cells and are pulled up by the round fitting atop the unit. (*IBM Corp.*)

dresses as they are needed. Afterwards, the operator removes the pack and returns it to the library.

Most disk units contain ten to thirty million bytes of information: in human terms, three thousand to nine thousand printed pages like this one. The speed of the memory is about the same as drum, on the order of 1/10 of a second.

Another mass memory system which is newer and less common than drum and disk is the *card memory*. This is sometimes also called *data cell storage*. Information is stored magnetically on stiff strips of material similar to plastic playing cards. Upon command, the system lifts the addressed card out of a file and reads or writes on it with heads like those on drums and disks. Card memory is slower than other auxiliary storage, from 1/10 to 6/10 of a second for a fetch cycle. However, the capacity is almost unlimited—billions of bytes per cell—and the cells can be changed even more easily than disk packs.

## Learned Memory

This is the basic knowledge the computer must have in order to work. When you tell the machine to add two numbers, for example, it refers to the learned memory (*software system*) to see what steps are required to do addition. The software tells the control unit to clear the accumulator, move one number into it from memory, move the other number to the adder, and so forth. Without the painfully explicit detail of these basic instructions, the computer simply cannot perform addition.

These elementary operations, called *routines*, are stored in one of two ways in most computers. One way is to have *firmware routines*. This means that there is an electronic circuit containing complete instructions for each routine. If a comparison is to be made, the control unit activates the responsible circuit. It takes over and issues all the instructions for moving data hither and yon, operating the logic unit and comparing the values. When the operation is completed, the circuit returns the command of the computer to the control unit.

Such firmware routines are actually a part of the control unit. Most times they are physically attached to plastic cards and plugged into racks in the CPU. In computers using mainly firmware routines, the control unit consists of hundreds of these cards and a central "traffic cop" that merely activates the routines in the order dictated by the program.

The other learned memory system uses core storage. The routines are stored in main core and read as needed by the control unit. Let's say the control unit reads the instruction $Z = X - Y$. Upon seeing the minus sign, it looks into core for the routine telling it each step to follow.

Because these routines are so vital to the computer's operation, they must be defended against the possibility of accidental erasure. The loss of any routine could be a disaster. For this reason, a special area in core is set aside to contain the learned routines. This area is called *protected core,* or sometimes *read-only memory*. Safeguards are built into the addressing routines to prevent the system from erasing or writing over its own learned memory. Thus the control unit can only read from the protected area, and can never write into that portion of core.

Many computers use a combination of firmware routines and protected core. Whatever methods are used, this learned memory is the basic intelligence of the computer. The routines usually can't be discarded or altered in any way without a physical modification of the computer equipment.

Until now we have limited our examination of the computer to its internal organs: logic, control, and memory. We know how it thinks, remembers, and learns.

But as we mentioned before, if you were as smart as a whole platoon of Einsteins but were unable to communicate, all that brilliance would be of no value. This is also true for the computer. High-speed computation and enormous storage capabilities mean nothing unless we can get the information into the system and it in turn can supply the answers.

# 8

# Eyes and Ears

You, a human, have five senses. You feel, hear, see, taste, and smell. Each of these senses has its own organ with which to perform. Feel: skin. Hear: ears. See: eyes. And so forth. Through the senses, you perceive the world about you. Each of them is a window with a different view, but they all serve the purpose of allowing information to pass from the outside to the inside. They are, in a word, inputs. The organs that do the sensing are your *input devices.*

The computer, as you know, is a machine in your image, but much more limited in every way (except speed) than you. In the area of senses especially, the computer is your inferior. It has not been given the senses it does not need. It does not feel someone's touch on its cabinets because touch in no way affects its operation. It doesn't taste because it consumes no food. It has no ability to smell since it doesn't breathe. There is no need for a computer to have these senses, so they are not built into it.

That leaves the senses of sight and hearing. Every

computer must have a set of specialized eyes. Some computers have ears, too, though hearing is not an absolute necessity. These are the only two senses with which a computer is equipped, because they are the only ones it needs.

The devices we will call eyes are the inputs attached directly to the computer. They read information recorded on a variety of sources and send what they read to memory. The ears listen to signals arriving over telephone lines from input machines across the hall or across the sea. What they hear they, too, send to memory.

The sources on which information is recorded are called *media*. A medium is a carrier of information. The media used with computers carry information recorded in such a way that the computer input devices can read it.

Before we begin examining the eyes and ears and the media they read, let's talk about making sense.

## Input Format

Suppose I say to you, "18529." What is your reaction? Anger? Terror? Bellowing laughter?

In all likelihood, your response to the message is something like, "So what? I haven't asked you a question and nothing was said to illuminate the deep and dark meaning of 18529. It might represent the number of hairs on the chin of a frog, or it might just as well be the number of portable sandblasters in the city of Sheboygan."

However, if you asked me, "How many words are there so far in this book?" and I answered "18529," then the number would be meaningful to you. The point is that any numerical statement must be defined in order to have meaning, because otherwise it is nonsense. Your input device "reads" it, but your processor hasn't the faintest idea what to do with it.

Now computers, as we have said, are idiots. Everything has to be spelled out in agonizing detail for them. You cannot forget one tiny detail or the computer will become totally bewildered. What's more, it will make no effort whatsoever to figure out what is wrong. So when we tell the computer anything, we must define what we are telling it. If we fail to do so, its reaction will be similar to yours when I unexpectedly presented you with a number.

There are rules and procedures for inputting information. These vary from one machine to another, and often one machine will have several sets of rules. There isn't room in this book to list all the different sets of rules, nor is it our intention to teach you to be a computer input specialist. There are, however, some general rules about data input, and those we will discuss.

First, as has been said, we must define for the computer what we are telling it. If it's a new program of instructions, we send a message like "NEW" which the computer recognizes as a code requiring certain conditions and actions on its part. If it is new data for an existing program, we tell it something like "NEW DATA" plus the program's name. There are many different methods used for telling the computer what it is about to read; all serve to define the information and tell the computer how to treat it.

Second, the input has to be organized in a certain way. This organization is called the *input format*. All computers have strict format requirements. For example, programs must be named and their instructions numbered in the order in which they are to be executed. No instruction may be more than so many characters in length. Data must be identified by a code word such as "$DATA" to tell the computer that what follows is not an instruction, etc. The purpose of such rules is not just to be unpleasant or to give the programmer a little added challenge, but rather to make it easy for the computer to decide what it is looking at and what to do with it. Remember, the computer has no initiative, so we should take care not to confuse it.

As for data such as groups of numbers, the format has to be specified exactly before the input begins. Data processing is beautifully suited for handling large amounts of the same kind of information, so long as the information is uniform.

Let's assume that we want the computer to tell us how many people between the ages of twenty and thirty, living in an area whose zip code begins with a 2, own three cars or more. (The program to process this data is already in memory.) First we collect these three items of information (age, number of cars, and zip code) for every car owner in the United States. We prepare it for input to the computer in the following format:

27120810

Then, before the input begins, we tell the computer that the data we are about to read into it is divided into three *fields:* two digits (age), one digit (number of cars owned), and five digits (zip code). Furthermore, we tell it to ignore the last four digits of the zip code since they are of no value to the problem. We begin to input this mass of data.

The computer has been told how the input data is formatted, so it knows what to do. It accepts each string of eight digits as read by the input device and writes them in core as they arrive. However, in moving the data on to auxiliary storage it breaks apart the strings according to the format rules we gave it. The first two digits (age) are sent to one area. The third digit (number of cars) is sent to another area in mass storage. The fourth digit (first number is the zip code) is written into yet another set of addresses. The remaining digits are to be ignored, so they are merely erased from core. Thus, the input is broken down like this inside the computer:

27   1   2   0̸8̸1̸0̸

When all the data has been read into the computer, the final step is to tell it, by some message the machine understands, that the input is finished. This is usually done with a word like "END" or a special end-of-block character. The computer is now ready to run the program whenever we tell it to do so.

The sample data we have used is easy to figure out since we know the format. That data represents a person twenty-seven years old who owns one car and lives in the town whose zip code is 20810. And, if presented in that way to the computer, it too will "figure out" the data. But let's say there is another twenty-seven-year-old, one-car owner in 20810's town, and that the person who prepared the data on him made a format error. The error is a reversal of the first two fields, so the data presented to the computer is 12720810. The computer will read this as a twelve-year-old with seven cars! No doubt the person who prepared the data knows just what he meant, but the computer doesn't. Without a moment's hesitation it will give a wrong answer to the problem.

This example shows us a great deal about the input of data. From it we can see what sort of rules apply to the format. It also shows how the data is treated after being read, and that some basic operations such as ignoring fields or parts of fields can be performed during input. Finally, it demonstrates one of the many possible consequences of incorrect format.

Now that we know something about what is being input and what happens to it from there, let's make a survey of the devices themselves.

## Input Devices

Your eyes are certainly the most advanced input devices in existence. They see almost everything large enough to be detected and pass this information on to your brain. They can read the letters on this page. They can also read handwriting, which is different than printing. If we punch the shapes of letters into a strip of paper they can read that too, and it's different than either printing or writing. Also your eyes find information in shapes and sizes and colors (how else do you recognize a friend's face, or the front of your house?) and they can judge distances, count objects, and measure quantities.

Computer eyes are not nearly as versatile as yours. In fact, they are very limited, so much so that each device can only see one thing. If we show a punched card to an input that can only read printed pages, the input will not recognize it. As we saw in the last section of this chapter, the data must be defined and organized in a format in order to be meaningful to the input devices that read it.

There are a number of inputs to computers. The types of inputs used by a machine are determined by the jobs the computer is expected to do. Many input devices are very specialized, as for instance magnetic ink character recognizers that read information from bank checks. Others are for general use.

Two of the most widely used general inputs are punched card readers and magnetic tape drives. These devices are so common we can say that all computers have them. They are the input workhorses of the data processing industry. Most of our attention in this chapter will be paid to them, although we will touch on others.

1. *Card readers.* Nearly everyone is familiar with the *punched card*. It is one of the most often-seen faces in modern America. People sometimes call it an IBM card. It is seen everywhere: in bills, in schools and colleges, in government offices, in businesses.

The punched card is a very simple medium. It is organized into eighty vertical columns and twelve horizontal rows. Each column represents one character of information. A character is coded onto the card by punching one row or more in a column. For example, if the format calls for the number 6 to appear in character position eleven, then row six of column eleven will be punched with a small rectangular hole. If we want to place an alphabetic letter, say a W, in the thirty-fourth character position, then column thirty-four will have punches in rows zero and six.

Note that this code structure is not the same as EBC-DIC. This is a twelve-bit code, not one of eight bits. The code used on punched cards is called the *Hollerith Code,* named after its inventor and the founder of the IBM Corporation, Herman Hollerith. Although the number and patterns of bits in Hollerith are different than in EBC-DIC, it is still a binary code. A punch is read as a 1 bit, the absence of a punch as a zero. One function of the card reader is to convert the Hollerith characters into EBCDIC or whatever code is used internally by the computer.

Keypunch machine. Cards feed down from hopper above keyboard, travel from right to left, and are collected in hopper on left. (*IBM Corp.*)

Cards are punched by a machine called, sensibly enough, a *card punch*. It is also called a *keypunch*. This machine is not a part of the computer, but rather is a device used to prepare data for the computer. It has a keyboard somewhat like a typewriter's. Cards feed from

a *hopper* into the *punching station.* As the human operator types, the machine punches the proper holes in the
card and advances the card to the next column. The operator does not have to know that a W is coded as punches
in rows 0 and 6. The machine automatically does this
when the W key is operated. When the card is punched
with all the data that belongs on it, it moves to another
hopper and a new card is brought to the punching station.
In this way, punched-card data is prepared for input. A
complete set of cards for a job is called a *deck.*

To input the deck we carry it to the computer's card
reader. The reader is an input device (''eye'') attached to
the computer by electrical wiring. There is a hopper on
the reader where the deck is placed. We turn on the
reader, but nothing happens. The computer hasn't yet
been told what to do.

Closeup of card punch keyboard. Punching station is the metal bar
above the switches. (*IBM Corp.*)

At the operator's console, we type a message to the computer telling it to input data with the card reader. The control unit takes over and instructs the reader to begin.

The reader takes the cards one by one from the hopper and runs them through the *reading station*. When a card is read, it is dropped into another hopper. Reading is done by one of two means. Some readers have pins that press against the card. If the pin passes through the card, there is a punch and the pin registers a 1 bit. If the pin cannot pass through, then there is no punch and a zero is read. The other means is by light. Light passes through a punched hole, where a photoelectric sensor reads a 1. The absence of light means there is no hole, so a zero is read. There is one pin or light sensor for each punch position in a character. A whole column is read at one time in both types of readers.

As the reader operates, it translates the Hollerith characters into the computer's internal language. The characters are then stored in a small memory called a *buffer*. Usually a buffer will hold three or four characters. When the buffer begins to get full, it tells the control unit. The control unit opens a path from the buffer into main storage and instructs the buffer to dump its contents at high speed. When the buffer is empty, the path is blocked and characters begin to collect in the buffer once again. Meanwhile, the data now in storage is identified by fields and sent on to auxiliary memory.

The buffer performs an important job. The internal speed of the CPU is thousands of times greater than the card reader's. Thus, while the reader plods along, the CPU can work on other jobs, pausing now and then to dump the buffer and tuck the input away for future use.

Again, as in the case of mass storage, the word "slow" is relative to CPU speed. Card readers do not seem slow to us people. A typical reader will handle fifteen cards per second. To keep up with it, you would have to read 12,000 words a minute.

2. *Magnetic tape.* Of all computer components, the mag tape unit (as it is called) is the most familiar to the greatest number of people. There are many who think this device *is* a computer. If you showed them a picture like the one here, they would identify it as a "computer," which, of course, it is not. It's no more than a large, special-purpose tape recorder.

Mag tape unit. About the size of a refrigerator. (*IBM Corp.*)

The mag tape unit is both an input and an output. The two functions come together in this component, so although this is a chapter on input we will also have to talk about mag tape output. If we did not we would be giving you half the story now and half later, and neither would satisfy your curiosity.

The tape drive is a refrigerator-sized cabinet. On its face are two reels, one to feed out tape, the other to take it up. In the travel from one reel to the other, the tape passes across a set of read/write heads like those used with drum and disk storage. The drive is connected to the CPU by electrical wiring.

The mag tape itself is a very long, narrow plastic strip. A reel usually contains 2,400 or 3,600 feet of tape a half-inch wide. The tape is coated with the same brown magnetic material found on drums and disks. Bits are recorded as tiny magnetized spots in a way now familiar to us because of our experience with auxiliary storage.

Characters are written across the width of the tape, usually in the same code used by the CPU. There is one read/write head for each bit position in the code. The *density*—that is, the number of characters per inch— varies from one drive to another. The most common densities are 556, 800, and 1,600 characters per inch. Thus one mag tape reel can hold from 16,000,000 to 89,000,000 characters of information, depending upon density and the length of the tape.

Mag tape, unlike its cousin auxiliary storage, is not addressable. The CPU cannot reach into the data on tape and grab a selected handful. For this reason, mag tape's usefulness is limited.

There is one kind of job, though, where it is hard to imagine any form of input/output that is superior to mag tape. This is where large quantities of *repetitive data* are involved. An example of repetitive data is personnel records on the employees of a business. For every employee there is a file set up in a standard format. It contains the employee's name, address, phone number, date of birth, Social Security number, salary, etc. This information is in fields, its only variation being the details pertaining to the particular employee. If we were going to commit the personnel records to mag tape, all we would have to do is establish the fields and their lengths (say 35 characters for the name, nine for the Social Security number, etc.) and record every file on mag tape according to the format rules. A whole library of computer programs could then be written to perform various tasks on the records.

Let's say our company has had a very successful year and the board of directors has just decided to give every employee a $50,000 raise. One employee, a fellow named Arthur Crabgrass, is responsible for this fantastic year, and he is being given a $100,000 raise in appreciation for his efforts. The personnel records on mag tape must be changed to show the new salaries.

The company has never done this kind of thing before, so no program now exists to do it. The programmer, however, is delighted to write one, since he gets a $50,000 raise too. He knows that the first field in the record format contains the employee's name and the sixth field is where the salary is recorded. With eagerly trembling hands, he writes a program instructing the computer to increase all salaries by $50,000 and lucky Arthur's by $100,000. This program is punched by the overjoyed keypunch operator and input to the computer. The mag tape containing personnel records is mounted on tape drive A and a blank tape is set up on drive B. The computer is told to run the job. Here's what happens:

The computer reads the first block of data by instructing the tape drive to input. The tape jerks past the read/write heads and is read. The data is sent into main core from the drive's buffer.

Field One is compared to the name Arthur Crabgrass. If the contents of that field arc not equal to (the same as) "ARTHUR CRABGRASS," the number 50000 is added to whatever quantity is shown in Field Six.

The control unit thcn tells tape drive B to write one block of data on tape. The record containing the new Field Six (salary) is sent from main core to the buffer in drive B. As the tape advances with a sudden jerk across

Mag tape drive closeup. Tape normally feeds from left to right. Read/write heads are in the small square enclosure between the reels. (*National Cash Register Co.*)

the read/write heads, the data is recorded on it. Meanwhile, another read-data command is sent from the control unit to drive A.

This process is repeated for every record on the tape. When the name in the first field is found to equal "ARTHUR CRABGRASS" the number 100000 is added to Field Six. Otherwise, all salaries are increased by 50000.

When the job is finished, the tapes are both rewound to the start position by the drives. The computer operators take time out from their rejoicing to dismount the tapes. The reel from drive B is now the company's official personnel records. It is stored in the tape library. The old tape is set aside to be used for some other purpose.

To carry this example a little farther, let's suppose a few days have now passed and the company's numerous and satisfied customers have sent in a bundle of new orders. These orders are to be stored on mag tape. The reel containing the old personnel records is mounted on one of the drives. Even though the tape still contains the old records, the computer runs the job and writes the order data on the tape. As it writes, the old personnel records are erased. When the job is finished, no one is saddened by the fact that there remains no trace of the old records on that tape.

There are several lessons to be learned from this example other than that this is a good company to work for. First, mag tape is well suited to repetitive tasks in which the same or similar things are done to many records. Second, we have seen how data processing works using mag tape. Third, mag tape drives, like card readers and all other input devices, have buffers. Last, the same reel of tape can be used over and over, and each time it is written on the old contents are destroyed.

One of the greatest advantages of tape over cards and other inputs is its speed. A slow drive will read 20,000 characters a second. Some run as high as 320,000. The average is about 60,000 characters per second. This is about 720,000 words per minute in human reading speed. That is still a long way from CPU speeds, but it's a lot closer than any other input or output.

Up until about 1967, mag tape was strictly limited to the computer. Only computers could write on it and only they could read what was written there. If new information was to be stored on tape, it first had to be punched in cards, then read into the computer. The computer would record it on tape. It costs hundreds and thousands of dollars per hour to run a computer. Everyone realized that it was expensive and a waste of valuable CPU time to go through these gymnastics to get data onto tape, but there was little choice. The computer people had to shrug and comfort themselves with the thought that tape is a better library medium—it is harder to lose a reel than a card, and more characters can be held in a small space on tape—and a faster input/output during processing, and that justified the expense.

Then in the 1960s there appeared the key-to-tape device. This machine is similar to a card punch except that it records data directly on mag tape. The operator types on the keyboard and a buffer stores up to a full block of information. The contents of the buffer can be checked for accuracy before they are written on the tape. To record the data, a button is pushed, the tape snaps forward and the buffer dumps onto read/write heads. Key-to-tape does away with the whole conversion process done by the computer before. For this reason it was an important development in the preparation of input data.

3. Other input devices. There is a whole multitude of inputs designed for special jobs. The number of computers equipped with these devices is low, but they're important nonetheless. The more common of these special-purpose inputs are paper tape readers and a group of machines called optical scanners, which read printed characters.

Key-to-tape device. Keyboard is the same as a keypunch. Data is recorded on tape over the operator's shoulder. (*Honeywell*)

*Paper tape* is usually a product of teletypewriter machines—typewriters that communicate over phone lines. As characters are received, the machine punches round holes across one-inch-wide paper tape. A hole represents a 1 bit, a no-hole a 0 bit, just as with punched cards. The tape, which may be hundreds of feet long, is rolled onto a reel, and mounted on the computer's *paper tape reader* much like mag tape.

The tape reader works in a way similar to card readers. In some machines, pins for each bit position press the tape as it travels across the reading station. If the pin goes through the tape, a 1 is read. If not, a zero is read. In more advanced, higher-speed readers, light shines on the tape and its passage or non-passage is sensed by photoelectric cells.

Tape readers range in speed from 100 to 1,000 characters per second. The advantage of paper tape is that input data can be prepared by a teletype operator far from the

**Punched Paper Tape**

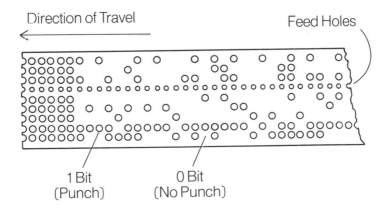

Direction of Travel

Feed Holes

1 Bit
(Punch)

0 Bit
(No Punch)

computer, sent to the data processing center and read into the computer with a minimum of handling and preparation. The disadvantages are that paper tape is messy to handle (it is lightly soaked with oil), it cannot be reused like mag tape, and it's hard to correct errors.

Paper tape reader. As with mag tape, feeds from left reel to right. Reading station is atop center box. (*National Cash Register Co.*)

*Optical scanners* come in a variety of flavors. They are truly eyes fitted to the computer, because they read information directly from paper. Optical scanners can be divided into three general classes: mark-sense, magnetic ink, and optical character recognition.

*Mark-sense cards* are used where humans must record repetitive data without expensive machinery. An example of such an application is in the telephone industry, where operators fill out tickets for some long-distance calls. The operator records details of the call (calling and called number, time of day, type of call, etc.) by marking ovals on the face of an IBM-type card. There is an oval for each type of information and, in some cases, for individual digits. These are marked with a lead pencil. They are periodically collected into a deck and sent to the data processing center. There they are run through a *mark-sense reader* which presses two pins against each oval and tries to pass electrical current through them. The lead pencil marks will allow the current to flow, thus enabling the reader to detect which ovals are marked. The program tells the computer what each marked oval means.

Mark-sense reading is also used on sheets of paper. An example of this is the General Educational Development tests given annually to public school students. Every question has, say, four possible answers with a box for each on the answer sheet. The correct box is marked with a lead pencil. The answer sheets are read by a mark-sense reader, which enables the computer to grade the papers.

*Magnetic ink character recognition* (MICR) is used throughout the United States by the banking industry. Every bank check is printed with MICR symbols along the bottom edge. These characters are readable both by humans and by MICR readers. They are used to identify the bank, the account in the bank on which the check is drawn, and the amount of the check.

The ink used has a tiny magnetic field. Since each character has a unique shape, its magnetic field has the same identifying shape. The MICR reader detects the meaning of the character by analyzing the field around it as it passes the read head. The reader then generates the proper binary character and sends it into the computer.

MICR is so popular with the bankers because it is extremely difficult to tamper with the characters. Dirt, pen marks, cross-outs, and changes have no effect on the shape of the magnetic field. If I should take one of your checks and cross out your account number, substituting mine for it, the MICR reader could still read your number. More importantly, if I change the bank identification number with a black pen so that it looks like another bank's (where I don't have an account and no one has ever heard of me), the MICR reader will not be fooled a bit.

*Optical character recognition* (OCR) is similar to MICR except that regular ink is used and the reader recognizes characters by their visual shapes, just as you do. OCR is one of the fastest-growing input means because, at least in theory, no special preparation is needed for input data. Any typed document that is reasonably clean and flat can be read and stored in memory.

In actual fact, the development of OCR is not that far along yet. Most OCR readers are limited to special letter shapes which are easily read by people even though they are not standard, garden variety typewriter letters. A lot of work is being done to perfect OCR, and a few readers are now available (at high cost and relatively low error reliability) that can accept standard type.

Some of the problems (engineers prefer to call them "opportunities" or "challenges") in OCR are variations in type size, style, and spacing (the difference between pica and elite type, for example), dirt and smudges on the copy, differences in paper quality and creases in the doc-

Optical Character Reader. Documents pass the light (pointed out by the operator), where printed characters are read. (*Honeywell*)

uments. Since OCR depends upon the contrast between the typed characters and the paper background, off-color paper and low reflectivity are also problems.

A brand new area within the new technology of OCR is handwriting recognition. This form of OCR input reads numbers and letters printed by hand in boxes on the medium. It is not possible to read cursive script (and probably never will be) because of the enormous differences in people's styles. However, characters carefully printed by hand can be read, and are.

The potential of OCR is huge. When OCR is perfected, any typed documents—books, letters, forms, memos, orders—will be acceptable computer inputs without further preparation.

## A Sense of Hearing

The computer is a stationary machine and, like a man in outer space, it needs a well-controlled place in which to function. Taken out of its comfortable little world it cannot survive.

Not only that, but computers are entirely too expensive to distribute to all areas needing their services. Take one large company as an example. It has offices in fifty major cities from New York to Los Angeles and from Miami to Seattle, plus ten factories and five warehouses. That is sixty-five locations, every one of which could use a computer. But the cost would be so great that the company would go broke if it gave a computer to each of them.

And so we creators of the electronic idiot have given it the ability to listen to telephone lines much as you do. In this particular company, one gigantic computer is located in the middle of the country, in Kansas City. The other sixty-four locations reach it by phone and in this way, one computer is extended from sea to shining sea without ever leaving the snug comforts of home. This is known as *data communications*.

Each location is equipped with an input/output device. These machines, of which there are an infinite number of types, read data in the same manner as the inputs attached directly to the computer, the "eyes." Then, over the phone lines, they tell the computer what they see.

The computer is equipped with a special input device

called a *Communications Control Unit* (CCU). The CCU has many "ears," ranging from four to over a hundred, depending upon need. Each "ear" is a buffer, to which a phone line is connected. Data may arrive simultaneously over several, or all, phone lines. As it comes in it is stored in the buffer connected to the line. The CCU periodically goes around to all the buffers and dumps their contents into main storage, keeping track of which buffer each piece of data came from. When the input is completed, the processor then reassembles all the pieces into their proper order and goes to work.

For output, the reverse takes place. The buffer is periodically loaded with data from main core. The buffer dumps onto the line at the speed of the distant output machine.

Data set (modem). Can be used as a normal telephone when "talk" button is operated. Data is transmitted by pressing "data" key. (*AT & T Co.*)

It makes little difference in the internal operations of the computer that the inputs and outputs involve data communications. Inside the machine, one input is about the same as any other.

The phone lines are equipped with special communications adaptors called *data sets.* Sometimes data sets are also called *modems,* a contraction of the terms *mo*dulator-*dem*odulator. The difference between a data set and a modem is the difference between a car and an auto: none. The purpose of a modem is to convert output binary pulses into tones which can be sent long distances over wire (*modulation*) and to change received tones back into pulses for machine consumption (*demodulation*). Pulses of direct current such as computer bits don't get very far over wire before they begin to go out of shape. In a couple of miles they are scarcely recognizable even to a computer. In another few miles there is nothing left of them. So the data set changes pulses and no-pulses into alternating current, which is similar to the signal

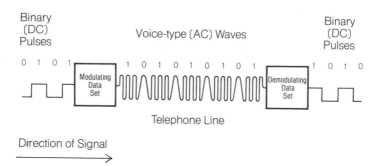

**Modulation and Demodulation
of Binary Signals for Transmission
of Data over a Telephone Line**

created on the line by the human voice. These AC signals will travel a long way over wire.

The input/output devices on the other end of the line from the computer are called *terminals*. There are, as we mentioned, jillions of terminals available, many more than there are of direct computer inputs. However, they do not differ much from the inputs we know already, with one exception: *keyboard machines*.

Keyboard machines are typewriters designed for data communications. They send and receive binary bits over phone lines, using data sets. An operator in Biloxi, Mississippi, can sit at a keyboard and type input to the computer in Kansas City. As the operator types, the machine prints just as any typewriter would, but at the same instant the characters are received and read by the computer's CCU. The computer can send messages back to the operator, who sees them printed as they are received at

Typical keyboard terminal. This machine communicates with a computer at about fifteen characters per second. (*IBM Corp.*)

the terminal. Thus a dialogue is possible between the computer and the faraway operator. This is called the *conversational mode;* a very useful tool in some cases.

For example, a clerk in the Biloxi sales office wants to enter a new order into the computer system. She calls the computer by dialing her data set, identifies herself by a coded input and tells the computer (by keying certain letters and numbers) that she is going to enter an order. The computer asks for the customer's name, which the operator types. If the computer knows the address for this customer, it asks for the first item on the order and the quantity; if not, it requests the address. When the ordered items are entered, the auxiliary memory can be searched to find out if they are in stock. If some are not, the computer will advise the operator, and perhaps provide a date when they will be available. The amount of the sale is computed and typed on the order form in the keyboard machine. If other information is needed—for example, credit information—the computer will request it. This is dialogue, or conversation, between Man and machine.

Keyboard devices are very popular as terminals. They are often fitted with other input and output equipment such as card punches and readers. Thus the keyboard itself serves as both a conversational input and a keypunching station. Big input jobs can be punched before the computer is called, then the cards are read over the phone.

The eyes of the computer have existed for as long as the computer itself has. Their sight is improving steadily through better technology. The ears are much newer, and data communications is the greatest explosion in the world of computers. The Bell Telephone System has found that the use of data communications increases by

Teletypewriter machine. Often used as a computer terminal. Note the paper tape punch and reader on the left side. (*Teletype Corp.*)

30 percent *every year*. Through data communications it is possible for a widespread company to extend the benefits of data processing to every location it serves, using a single computer. Compared to computer costs, phone lines are as cheap as last year's Christmas trees. The use of rapid data communications has given rise to new computer uses. One very successful outgrowth of communications is computer time-sharing, in which many low-speed terminals can use one high-speed computer at the same time. Another is real-time processing, in which much of a firm's routine paper shuffling is replaced by instantaneous electronic notification of activities such as orders placed or shipped. Computer ears are going to continue to grow in usefulness and in number for a long time.

# 9

# Hands and Mouth

THE REASON—the *only* reason—for the existence of the computer is to get an output from it. To most of us, the input is not especially important so long as the computer gets the data accurately, without too much fuss and bother, and knows what to do with it once it has it. Likewise, to the majority of people, the internal activities of data processing—CPU, memory, decisions, and so forth—are of little more than casual interest. It all happens so fast that we cannot truly comprehend it, and unless we have written the program we haven't the faintest idea what miracles are occurring in the bat of an eye inside those expressionless boxes. But the output is very important to us all. If the output is wrong or it does not meet our needs, then the computer hasn't done its job and it may as well not even exist.

Your main output devices are your hands and your mouth. You write with your hands. You also perform tasks directed by your brain, such as the tying of shoes, and these activities are a form of output. With your mouth, of course, you talk, putting the results of your mental processing into terms others will understand.

The computer has outputs that can be compared to hands and a mouth. The hands, we can say, are the devices that print letters and numbers on paper. They also draw pictures, run factory machinery, mix bread dough and steer airplanes. The mouth has to do with data communications. It tells terminals what to write, or what to do with their hands. It also speaks with a human voice directly to people.

There is much in common between inputs and outputs. Some inputs we have talked about are also outputs— namely mag tape drives and keyboard devices—so we needn't discuss them further. Other outputs like page printers have no input capabilities, but they share characteristics with inputs. All are slower than the CPU, are buffered, and work under control of the computer. Their purpose is to enable Man and his marvelous moron to communicate.

## Page Printers

Upon entering a computer room one of the first things you notice is the page printer. This is a large component with paper spilling out its top and over the back. It is a noisy thing, whining and clicking as it pours out information.

Page printers come in two types: drum and chain. Both are used for the same purpose, which is to print out large volumes of information from memory. The type, drum or chain, is determined by the preferences of the manufacturer. Neither is better than the other, though drums hold the speed record.

*Drum printers* should not be confused with drum

storage, for they are not the same. The drum printer, like
the memory, takes its name from a large cylinder rotating
rapidly inside its works, but here all similarity ends. The
printer drum has strips of letters along its length, one letter for each position to be printed. Each strip contains all
the same letter. Most computer *printouts* have a max-
imum line length of 132 characters, so each strip has 132
of the same character. There is a strip of 132 A's, another of 132 B's, another of 132 C's, and so on. The
drum has at least one strip of 132 characters for each
symbol that can be printed.

Facing the drum is a row of 132 small hammers, one
for each print position. The paper feeds up between the
hammers and the drum, which is spinning at high speed.
If the letter A is to be printed in the fourth, ninth, and
eighty-third positions, the hammers for those positions all
strike the paper simultaneously when the A strip is opposite. This drives the paper against the drum and causes
the A's to be printed. Thus, all the A's in the line of type
are printed at once. Next the machine prints all the B's,
then all the C's and so on until every character in the line
is printed. Then the paper advances one line and the process begins all over again.

This sounds like a slow and clumsy operation, but it's
not. Drum printers are capable of speeds up to 1,500
lines per minute, which is equal to about 100 pages in a
book.

*Chain printers* also have a hammer for each print position. However, instead of a drum, there is a continuous
chain rather like a bicycle's turning on the other side of
the paper from the hammers. Each link in the chain contains one printable character. The entire set of characters
is usually repeated five times.

Computer page printer. Paper feeds up out of a bin in the lower front and collects in a rack on the rear side. (*National Cash Register Co.*)

As the chain moves, it carries the characters along the length of the row to be printed. If an R is to be printed in the fortieth position in the row, the hammer at that position strikes the paper as an R passes. This drives the paper against the R and prints it. Unlike drums, then, chain printers do not print all the letters of a certain type at the same time. Instead they print the characters as they pass the place where they are to appear.

Chain printers are not as fast as drums, but you wouldn't call them slow. Speeds go up to about 1,000 lines per minute, two-thirds the speed of drums.

Both chain and drum printers use a technique called line-at-a-time printing. The devices take entire lines of output and print the characters without respect to the order in which we read them. The first character to be printed in a line may well be the last to be read. This is different from a typewriter, which prints in the order of reading. The reason for line-at-a-time printing is that it is so much faster.

## Card Punches

Another very common computer output is punched cards. Most machines that have card readers also have punches. These are not the keyboard-type punches we talked about in the last chapter. Rather, they are actual components working under the direction of the control unit.

Page printer take-up rack, showing computer printout. (*Honeywell*)

Information to be punched is read out of main memory into the buffer in the punch. The punch then translates the computer code into Hollerith and punches cards as they are automatically fed through the punching station.

Some components combine the reading and punching operations into one machine known as a reader/punch. These devices share a buffer, code convertor, and other parts.

The speeds of card punches range from a hundred to five hundred cards per minute. If this book were being punched, the rates would be three to sixteen full pages a minute.

Computer punches do not print on the cards. Their only purpose is to punch holes. If printing is needed (as for example when bank checks are written on punched

Combined card reader/punch. (*National Cash Register Co.*)

cards to be used as turnaround documents) the cards are run through a machine called an *interpreter* after the computer is finished with them. The interpreter reads the holes and prints what they say on the card.

One of the handiest uses for computer card punches is in the creation of *turnaround documents*. An example was just cited in the last paragraph. Another example of a turnaround document is the punched card that comes with telephone bills. As the computer prints the phone bills, it also punches cards. These cards identify the customer and show the amount due. They are printed by an interpreter and combined with the printed bills to be sent out. In paying his bill, the customer returns the card with the money. As payments are made, the computer is fed these cards. They are matched against the computer files that created them. In this way the computer, and the telephone company, can keep track of the bills. A turnaround document, then, is defined as a card created by the computer as an output, sent out of the computer room, and returned later as an input.

## Paper Tape Punches

As with card equipment, paper tape components may be combined into reader/punches, or they may be separated. Paper tape is usually employed when the computer user operates a communications system of teletypewriters.

The computer produces messages that can be printed on a teleprinter machine. These messages are punched into inch-wide paper tape by the punch, which works much like the card punch. When a message is output by

Paper tape punch. Blank tape feeds from the left reel, is punched below the L-shaped enclosure, and moves to the take-up reel. (*National Cash Register Co.*)

the computer, the operator tears it off the machine and sends it out on a teletypewriter.

Most punches are slow in comparison to other computer outputs. Their speed is around 100 characters per second, or stated another way, about 1,000 words a minute.

## Skilled Hands

All the components we have just discussed, plus the mag tape drive, are the "handwriting" devices of the computer. They are the most common outputs, since one or more of them are found in every computer room. But they are by no means the only hands the computer has.

An engineer working on the design of a car motor can take advantage of the computer's ability to draw. If he needs a part to perform some particular job in the motor, he can tell the computer the requirements of the part—how big it should be, what it must do, what kinds of parts it will work with—and the computer will design and draw a picture of it. The drawing is made with a machine called a *plotter*.

Most plotters have a smooth drum. The paper wraps around this drum. There is a pen on a slide which moves from one side of the drum to the other. It can be raised away from the paper to be moved without marking, and lowered against it when a line is to be drawn. Under the computer's control the drum is turned back and forth, carrying the paper under the pen. At the same time the pen slides to and fro as directed. By varying the speed of motion of the drum and pen, the plotter can draw curves and straight lines, write, make circles, and do anything else a person normally does on paper.

Plotters are used for many different jobs. One is to draw contour maps in which terrain is represented by lines showing intervals of 100 feet in elevation. Such maps are used to detect landforms indicating oil deposits, ancient cities, and watershed problems. Another very common use of the plotter is to draw weather maps. Road builders use plotters to tell them how to route a new highway, and the computer can even tell them how to grade the hills and how much earth they must move. The Federal Government has devised a road design system using a three-dimensional plot. The drawings show the

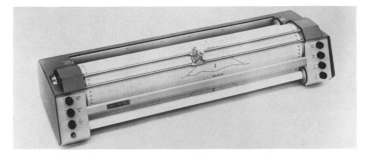

Typical drum plotter. Drum rotates, moving paper up and down. The pen is within the fitting at the center of the paper. It moves to and fro on the rods. The combination of motions produces the drawings. (*Calcomp*)

topography as it is now from the perspective of an airplane some distance above and away from the area, and as it will appear after the road is completed. This aids in determining the environmental impact of the project.

From the drawing of a part, it is but a short step to the making of it. This is called *process control*. A computer is placed in charge of one or more machines and told to make a complex part such as the cylinder block of an auto engine. It works with little or no human help, moving the part about, flipping it upside down, drilling, polishing, milling, and turning out a finished engine block. Parts made using process control are more accurate and flaw-free than human-made parts, and they can be turned out more quickly.

Process control is a form of computer output, just as the tying of your shoe is a form of output from you. The concept of process control can be extended to include the automatic control of a rocket launching at Cape Kennedy by computers in Greenbelt, Maryland, or to the automation of an entire oil refinery, or to the throwing of far-

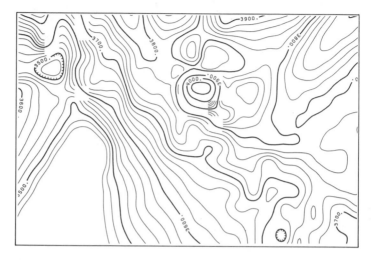

Plotter drawings. The upper drawing is a contour map showing elevations at 100-foot intervals. The lower is a three-dimensional projection of terrain. (*Calcomp*)

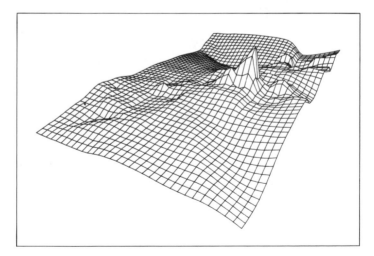

flung switches in remote mountains to divert electric power away from low-usage areas into high-demand cities, or to the automatic systems which fly the giant Boeing 747 airliner with humans doing little more than monitoring. All of these outputs are the results of CPU activities based upon inputs.

## The Voice of the Computer

In the last chapter we examined data communications. Terminals talk to computers, and the computers talk back, usually over the same phone connection. Before discussing this burgeoning field further, we must make a couple of observations. First, terminals are not limited to keyboard machines, card readers, punches, and other "nonintelligent" equipment. A terminal might be another computer, say a small machine acting as a high-speed input/output for a larger computer. Or it may be a large computer calling on another computer for assistance. Such aid is usually to help handle unusually heavy processing loads or to provide information stored in the second computer's memory. Sometimes, also, one computer will act as a *message switcher,* relaying information among a number of terminals and other computers. The second observation is that the language of such conversations is always in binary-type codes, which are meaningful to machinery but not to people. Thus, in data communications some piece of equipment must always act as a translator between Man and machine.

That can be a problem. Terminals are not expensive when compared to computers, but they aren't cheap either. About the lowest-cost keyboard terminal, including the data set and the phone line, rents for seventy-five or eighty dollars a month. At that rate not even the biggest, richest corporations can afford to provide all their employees with a terminal. Another thing about terminals is that they are fairly large and fragile, so that it is not practical to move them around or to provide them to salesmen and others who travel.

These problems have given the engineers further "opportunities" and led to the development of a brand of data communications called DIVA (pronounced DEE-va). DIVA stands for *D*igital *I*nput *V*oice *A*nswerback. The computer is outfitted with a special communications controller known as an *Audio Response Unit*. A number of phone lines can be connected to this unit, with each line having a pair of buffers at its disposal. One buffer receives incoming signals. The other converts binary-type

Telephone with pushbutton dial. Each row and each column of buttons generates a different tone. The combination of two tones signifies a digital value. The * and # on either side of the 0 are used in DIVA systems. (*AT & T Co.*)

characters from the computer into words spoken by a voice which sounds human, and sends these words out over the line.

The terminal in a DIVA system is usually a normal everyday telephone with a pushbutton dial. This kind of phone has twelve buttons, the ten digits plus two special symbols, arranged in a matrix of four rows by three columns. Each row and each column has its own tone. Any button depressed will generate two tones—the row tone and the column tone—which can be recognized as a combination meaning, say, a 2 or an 8. The input buffers on an Audio Response Unit can hear these tones and convert them into the binary characters used by the computer.

To see how all this fits together, let's say you're a bank teller. Arthur Crabgrass has now gotten that $100,000 pay raise and put it into his account with your bank. He comes to your window and asks to withdraw $10,000 from his account. That is a lot of money, and you want to be certain that he's not trying to "put one over on you." So you pick up the receiver and, using the pushbutton dial, tap out the phone number of the Audio Response Unit. The computer answers, "Account Balance System. Enter account number."

You operate the dial buttons, keying in Arthur's number. At the end of the number, you depress one of the special symbols to signal the end of input. The computer reads the account number out of the buffer and says, "Account number 98765." You compare this with the numbers you keyed in to make sure it's correct. Next the computer tells you, "Enter amount."

Again with the buttons, you input 10000 and the end-of-input symbol. The computer repeats the amount so you can check for accuracy; meanwhile it is comparing the input with the balance shown in the bulging Crabgrass account. The final decision is, "Withdrawal approved."

You hang up, numbed with awe, and give Arthur his money.

DIVA has a great many uses. Department stores depend on it for checking credit when a customer wants to charge a purchase. Hospitals have treatment plans on computer files so that a doctor can call, input certain information on the patient's condition, and receive instructions on how to treat the case. Salesmen call in orders from any pushbutton pay phone immediately after they are received from customers. Mathematicians key in a few numbers and instantly receive the answer to a complex equation. More new uses are found for DIVA every day. Its advantages are obvious: Any pushbutton telephone anywhere is an input device, and the output is directly and immediately understandable to people. There are disadvantages too, of course; input and output speeds are very low, and error rates are high. But in situations where the amount of information exchanged is small, DIVA is hard to beat.

## Display

Another important type of input/output terminal is the *data display device*. Usually computer people, in their love for mysterious jargon, will refer to it as a CRT. This term (in which the letters are pronounced individually) comes from *C*athode *R*ay *T*ube, which is the screen on which the display is projected.

In appearance a CRT resembles (and actually *is*) a small television set with a keyboard. As the operator types or as output is received from the computer, the characters are displayed on the screen through an elec-

Alphanumeric CRT terminal. Keyboard is similar to a typewriter's. (*IBM Corp.*)

tronic process that makes them glow against a dark background.

Part of the "guts" of a CRT is a buffer memory which stores the entire contents of one or more screens of information. This memory is very flexible, so that the operator can insert and remove individual characters or entire lines on the display. When the message is ready to be sent, the operator dumps the buffer onto the line. The answer comes back from the computer and is stored in the buffer, from which it is then written on the screen at high speed.

There are two types of CRT's: alphanumeric and graphic. The *alphanumeric CRT*, as its name suggests, displays letters and numbers on the screen. These charac-

ters are arranged in rows and columns. Because there is
no carriage or typing mechanism to show the operator
where the next character he keys will appear, a small
rectangle called a *cursor* is provided. When a character is
typed, it appears where the cursor is and the cursor
moves one position to the right. The cursor can be moved
up, down, right, or left, and "re-homed" at the upper
left corner of the screen. The entire display can be erased
if desired.

These CRT's come with a variety of options. For example, a user can buy what is called *protected format.*
This is similar to the protected core in main memory. Information stored in the buffer with protected format cannot be erased or changed unless a special procedure is
followed. Uses for this option are such things as headings
for items in sales forms, so that an operator merely fills
in the blanks as she might on a printed form prepared by
typewriter. Another common option is a page printer,
which enables the operator to get a printed copy of the
display.

The alphanumeric CRT is popular for several reasons,
one of which is its silence. This makes it suitable for office use. Another is that it needs no paper (unless there is
a printer with it), and it produces no unnecessary page
copy to clutter the place and jam the trash cans. A third is
that it is much faster than printer-type keyboard machines, usually operating at 1,200 to 2,400 words per
minute versus the average 135 of a printer.

Without doubt, the most fascinating terminal in use
today is the *graphic CRT.* This terminal, while differing
little in appearance from an ordinary alphanumeric CRT,
is one of the most sophisticated (and expensive) gadgets
to grow in the furrow cut by the computer.

The graphic CRT displays pictures drawn electronically on the screen by a computer. The screen is usually quite large, allowing for a good deal of sharp detail. In this aspect it is similar to a plotter, but the resemblance ends right where it begins. This picture is "alive." By operating controls on the CRT console, the drawing can be rotated in any direction, giving a moving three-dimensional picture of the object displayed. This allows an engineer working on housings for jet engines, for instance, to "handle" the housing he has had the computer design for him. He can turn it over and study its other side, roll it around, watch the contours for good aerodynamic lines, and examine any other part of it.

As if that weren't enough, the graphic CRT strides another mile with an attachment called a *light pen*. This is a pen-shaped affair wired to the CRT. If the engineer wants to reshape the airscoop on the housing, he "draws" on the screen with the light pen, sketching in the new lines over those displayed. These changes are read by the cathode tube and relayed to the computer, which redraws the picture in a few seconds. He can continue to tinker with the housing until he is satisfied with it, then have the computer actually draw plans for it on a plotter.

In the photo of the graphic CRT the engineer is showing us another use for this terminal. He is an electrical engineer working on computer circuit design by sketching the circuit layout with a light pen. When it is laid out he will assign values to the components (ohms to resistors, farads to capacitors, volts to power supplies, etc.). Then he will tell the computer what sort of signal is going to be input to the circuit. The computer will calculate the output signal based upon the component values. If this isn't what is needed, the engineer can change the values of any of the parts and the computer will automati-

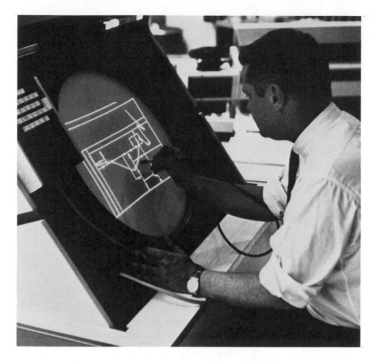

Graphic CRT terminal. Engineer is using a light pen to sketch in changes in an electronic circuit designed by the computer. (*Control Data Corp.*)

cally adjust the output calculations. This continues, changing values, perhaps adding or removing parts, until the design is satisfactory.

Such applications speed up engineering immeasurably. In a matter of a few minutes this electrical engineer can design a circuit and prove its design, all on the scope of the CRT. Only a few years ago he would have spent days on calculations, perhaps a week building the real circuit and many hours testing it.

This is one very specific example of how the computer has lent jet propulsion to technological advance.

# 10

# Directing an Idiot

THE COMPUTER IS unquestionably the most advanced, complex, and intelligent single tool Man has ever created. It does things in seconds that we would have thought impossible *ever* to accomplish a few years ago, and it does them so extraordinarily well that even those whose professions depend upon the computer tend to forget the one thing that Man must never forget: the computer is a complete, blithering idiot.

This magnificent creation is wholly and utterly dependent upon people. It is more obedient than the best-trained soldier, and has less imagination and initiative. It is a more powerful tool than the hydrogen bomb, and yet it is more helpless than the tiniest infant. It can be turned to the most perplexing problems of mankind and yield brilliant answers, yet it has no sense of values, no morality, and no insight.

In a marvelous article in *Life* magazine dealing with the question of machine "thought," Robert Campbell summarizes the personality of the computer.

A computer . . . can pay undivided attention to details
that would drive a mortal right out of his mind. It can be
told something and won't forget it until told to do so. It
never gets huffy. It will work on the most boring problem
forever without getting overheated. It will not laugh out-
right at human error and will work prodigiously at any
problem put to it, no matter how trivial.*

Nowhere is this simple-mindedness more clearly seen
than in computer programming. To tell a computer how
to do a job is to direct an idiot. Every tiny detail must be
painstakingly explained, no matter how obvious it may
seem to a human. The computer does not learn from experience, so even though it may have done one million
and seven problems all exactly the same, the million and
eighth time it has to be told all over again precisely how
to do the job.

Computer people have a useful word to describe this
moronic characteristic: GIGO. GIGO is derived from the
phrase *G*arbage *I*n—*G*arbage *O*ut, meaning that the
wrong input will invariably produce the wrong output. If
someone asks you, "Three calendars plus four sugar-
lumps equals how many steering wheels?" you would no
doubt sense that something was wrong (most likely with
the person who asked such a question). The computer
would not. It would say seven (so long as it had been told
to add the two digits) and never even pause to consider
how ridiculous the whole problem is.

Because the computer has no ability to judge what it is
doing, it is our responsibility as the directors of the idiot
to give directions in such a way that the job is done properly. A computer is only as good as its programmer. Gar-

* "The Eerie Interface of Man and Machine" by Robert Campbell. *Life.*
63:72. October 27, 1967.

bage as input produces garbage as output. And output is
the computer's only product.

A *computer program* is a set of instructions that tells
the computer how to solve a problem. A "problem" can
be anything from adding two digits to launching a rocket.
The program must be organized into a logical sequence
leading from start to finish, with each step numbered in
the order in which it is to be done.

For an example, we are going to dust off our old
friend, the sample problem from Chapter 4. You are a
computer programmer who has a machine equipped with
a page printer. Your job is to program the equation:

$$F = \frac{(A \times B) - (A + B)}{B}$$

The answer is to be output on the printer.

After studying the formula for a moment, you see that
it can easily be broken down into several steps. To help
plan the program, you draw a *flowchart* showing each
step. The events are connected with arrows to indicate
their order. (See illustration on page 120.)

You check the flowchart for accuracy of the reasoning
(the lesson hidden within the lesson is that the programmer must know how to solve the problem before he can
tell the computer how to do it). This is a workable program; all the steps are there for this job, nothing is miss-
ing and you aren't trying to use some value that hasn't already been computed by the time it is needed. Now you
code the actual program for input:

```
 5 READ A
10 READ B
15 LET C = A * B
```

20 LET D = A + B
25 LET E = C − D
30 LET F = E / B
35 PRINT F
40 STOP

You punch the program in cards, one instruction per card, and input it. The computer saves it in auxiliary storage. Now you have a program that will find F for any two numbers assigned to A and B. To test your program, you call it into main core and input a card:

45 DATA 9,3

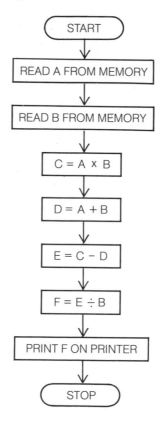

The numbers 9 and 3 are stored in memory as data inputs. The word DATA in this step is not an instruction to be acted on by the computer. Rather, it is an identifier to tell the computer what the following numbers are. The comma is a field separator.

At the console you tell the computer to RUN. The computer executes the instructions in their numeric order, ignoring the fact that they are numbered by fives. It knows that it is supposed to look for the next-higher numbered command each time it completes an instruction.

The first step tells it to READ A. It looks at the data inputs in memory and assigns the name A to the first value it finds: in this case, to 9. The next step says to READ B, so the name B is given to the 3. For step 15, the numbers 9 and 3 are moved to the arithmetic unit and multiplied. The result is stored in a location which the control unit names C. So it goes until the answer, 5, is printed.

That is a very easy problem. Even the computer, for all its stupidity, would agree that it doesn't take a lot of talent to run it. So let's have the electronic brain cells work a little harder and make a decision. Instead of always dividing by B in the last computation, we'll have it divide by the lower of the two values we input. That way we humans can be our usual sloppy selves and not worry about whether we input 3 and 9 or 9 and 3. (See illustration on page 123.)

This sequence of events is the same as in the other program until we have found the value of E. Now we have to compare A and B and make a decision. If A is bigger (if $A = 9$), then we divide by B. If B is the larger ($B = 9$), we go the opposite way and divide by A, which is obviously the smaller number. Whichever, we have to

print F, so either choice leads us back to that instruction.
Now we code the program:

```
 5  READ A
10  READ B
15  LET C = A * B
20  LET D = A + B
25  LET E = C − D
30  IF A > B THEN 45
35  LET F = E / A
40  GO TO 50
45  LET F = E / B
50  PRINT F
55  STOP
```

Things happen just as before through step 25. But then
let's say that at step 30, it is found that A is greater than
B (A = 9). The computer jumps to step 45 and divides E
by B (3), which is obviously smaller than A. Then it goes
on to 50. On the other hand, if step 30 finds that A is *not*
greater than B (A = 3), it merely "falls through" to the
next instruction in 35. There E is divided by A, which
has been proven to be smaller. Step 40 tells the computer
to jump to 50, bypassing the other choice in step 45
without so much as a sidelong glance.

Under this arrangement of instructions, no matter
whether we input our data as 9 and 3 or as 3 and 9, we
will always come up with 5 as the value for F. When we
input the data, then, we can either say:

```
60  DATA 3,9      or
60  DATA 9,3
```

and it won't make the slightest difference.

One of the most useful things a computer does is to process a large amount of information, performing the same operations over and over on repetitive data. Remember that generous company that gave all its employees the $50,000 raise? Well, let's use a flashback and return to the point where the company had just decided to do it. We have to produce a printed list for the boss showing everyone's name, age, old salary, and new salary.

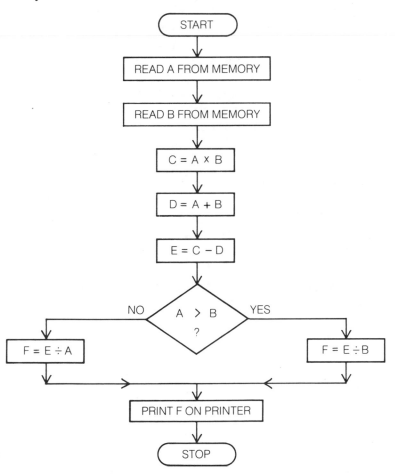

First, let's make some rules. The old salary records are in main core. The fields are the employee's name, age, and present wages. The computer's drum printer will be used to print the list. There are 1,000 employees. (See flowchart on opposite page.)

Before we go on with this problem, let's pause a moment and look at the flowchart. Note a couple of things about it. First, symbols are used to denote different kinds of actions. A rectangle is a process of some sort, for example, telling the computer that the increase is $50,000, or adding the increase to the old salary to produce the new. A diamond is a decision, from which there are two possible outcomes labeled YES and NO. Second, arrows are used to show the direction of further activity. At the step for comparing the counter to 1,000, for example, the YES arrow indicates that if the outcome of the decision is that the counter is equal to 1,000, then we go to the STOP command because all the employees have been processed. If, on the other hand, the decision is NO, then we return to the start of the process and follow the arrows and decisions back down again. These are standard flow-charting symbols used by programmers. The advantage of using such commonly recognized symbols is that anyone who knows anything about programming can follow a programmer's logic. In this way, if a programmer takes advantage of the career opportunities discussed in the back of this book, the fellow who replaces him can figure out the workings and reasoning of the programs he wrote.

Going back to the problem now, we check over the flowchart to make sure the program is going to be correct. It is always essential that it be correct, but in this case it's especially important since such a handsome raise is involved, and this report is for the boss. The computer has been told how much the increase is. A counter has

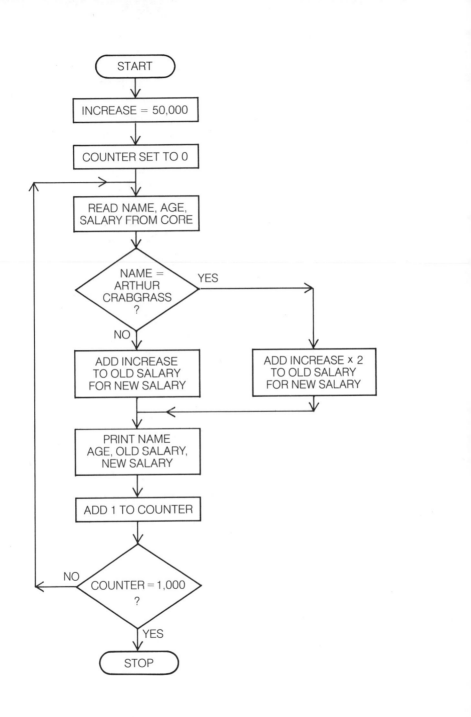

been set up to keep track of how many times the process is repeated. We have told it what to read. If the record is Arthur's (to whom we owe our thanks), twice the increase is added to his salary. Otherwise only the paltry $50,000 is added. In either case, the next step is to print all the information. Finally, the counter increases by 1. If it shows less than 1,000, we loop back to the READ step, read the next record and repeat the process. When the counter reaches 1,000, the job is finished.

Now that we know the logic of the program will work, we code it into instructions for the computer:

```
 5 LET I = 50000
10 LET C = 0
15 READ NE, A, S
20 IF NE = ARTHUR CRABGRASS THEN 35
25 LET N = S + I
30 GO TO 40
35 LET N = S + (I * 2)
40 PRINT NE, A, S, N
45 LET C = C + 1
50 IF C = 1000 THEN 60
55 GO TO 15
60 STOP
```

Note that each value has been given a name: I for the increase, C for the counter, NE the name of the employee, A his age, S his old salary, N the new. These names symbolize values to us humans. The computer regards them as memory locations. It couldn't possibly care less what those symbols stand for; it only needs the names so it can know where to look when the instruction stating them is executed.

Steps 20 through 35 are a decision and its two possible results. If the name of the employee is Arthur Crabgrass, steps 25 and 30 are skipped. If it's not, 25 and 30 are done and 35 is bypassed.

Down at line 45, the old reading for C is increased by 1 to make a new C reading. The LET command tells the computer that the value to the left of the equals sign is the answer to the computation to the right of it. In this instruction (number 45), if the old value for D is 314, then 314 will be moved out of the memory address called C into the accumulator. A 1 will be added to it and the new value, 315, will be stored at the same address.

In step 50, C is compared to 1,000. If they are equal, we jump to the STOP command and cease the execution of the program. If not, we return to step 15. When this happens, the computer reads the next record. Notice one thing: The names of the data fields are the same with every repetition—NE, A, and S. The computer, however, does not read the same record over and over. It remembers where it read the last record and goes to the next one every time it executes a READ. In this case, it gives the next three addresses the names NE, A, and S in that order. From then on every time those names are mentioned in the program, the computer looks at those locations until the next READ, when the following three addresses are named NE, A, and S. This is why it is so important to follow the input format rules. If a careless operator were to twist around the positions of the age (A) and salary (S), the computer wouldn't hesitate to believe that a man 17,000 years old makes $34 a year!

## Killing the Bugs

The purpose of this book is to familiarize you with computers in general, not to make you a programmer.

However, no discussion of programming would be more than half complete without a few words on the agonies of debugging.

A "bug" in computerese is an unexpected problem either in the equipment or in a program. Most often it is some tiny mistake somewhere that causes things to go terribly sour just about the time you begin to congratulate yourself on a superb job.

I'm going to draw from my own personal experience to give you an example of a "bug." I once wrote a program that takes the number of characters of information being sent among any number of cities up to a hundred and computes long distance costs to transmit them. It took about a day to write the program and get it into the computer. There were a few errors to be corrected, as there always are. By day's end, though, the program was all corrected and set to use—or so I thought.

For several days I used the program occasionally to help design a data communications system I was working on, and never encountered a single problem. Then one day some people (including my boss) came to watch this wonderful new program in action. At the time I had a real problem to give to the computer and so, filled with pride, I input the data. Dutifully the computer chewed up the data and began spitting out the answer. Everyone huddled over the printer in admiration, casting secret glances at me that were filled with worship for the mastery of the computer. (I am always amazed at the adulation people heap on those who make the computer work.) I was beginning to feel the first tingles of that $50,000 raise. And of course, that was when the bug bit.

Two towns, some ten miles apart in reality, were suddenly electronically uprooted and moved 953,564 miles

away from one another; about four times as far away as
the Moon. Everything else worked perfectly, but that
didn't save my dignity. The program was obviously, and
very publicly, wrong.

Immediately I had the program and the data printed out
and went to work on it. Four eye-blurring and reputation-
destroying days later, the bug was found; one character in
a very simple instruction was wrong. That step had probably never been done until the embarrassing moment.

A bug in a NASA program a few years ago makes all
other bugs seem tiny by comparison. A giant rocket lifted
from Cape Kennedy and, in computer-controlled majesty,
began its voyage to the planet Venus. Five minutes after
leaving Earth, it went violently out of control and created
a fireworks show worth $19 million. The cause: a forgot-
ten hyphen in the midst of millions of flawless instructions.

These two examples again point out what we have
stressed all along: The computer is an idiot. It does what
it is told to do and if the instructions are wrong, it performs accordingly. Fortunately, most bugs are on a small
scale, similar to mine, and not on the gigantic order of
NASA's. They always come out, sooner or later (I know
of one that didn't show up for four years). When they do,
it's like trying to find that penny you dropped in the tall
grass.

## Across the Language Barrier

You may not realize this, but your mind does not think
with words. Its work is done with images, emotions, sensations you've stored. Take the word Christmas as an

illustration. Immediately it brings to mind images of a tree, bright colors, sensations of pleasure, perhaps a certain excitement. These are associations which mean Christmas to you. The word itself is only a collection of sounds (or letters symbolizing the sounds) that trigger the associations. Thought, by and large, is a process of arranging these associations into complex patterns. Words, on the other hand, are vehicles by which information comes to you and leaves you.

Human language is not an efficient means of conveying information. We haven't found a better one yet, but that is because we have developed this means to conform to our own capabilities and limitations. Within the scope of the human are the muscular structures for articulating a variety of sounds and for hearing and interpreting them. Besides, our language suits us quite well because we humans are not especially efficient creatures. I can say to you, "I go buy." and you will understand what I mean. But it sounds more human, and definitely *is* less efficient, for me to say, "I'm going to go shopping."

However, just because it is our nature to be inefficient doesn't mean that we cannot understand and use the rules of logic and efficiency. That is Man's genius, and it is the very trait that enabled us to invent the computer, a machine built upon those rules. Logic, efficiency, and the speed that comes from their use are what the computer has to offer us.

For this reason, it would make little sense to have the computer do its "thinking" with inefficient human words. It *does* make sense for the computer to respond to associations of its own kind.

This is all well and good for computers, but it creates difficulties for the people who are trying to communicate their wishes to the computer. It's a language barrier, just like the language barrier separating you, the English speaker, from Mehmed, who speaks only Turkish.

During the early years of the computer's life, however, people had no choice but to contend with this language problem as best they could. Programming was a horribly complicated job which only the bravest and most dedicated could tolerate for very long. Not only were the techniques of programming primitive and difficult but this new means of problem-solving presented a coding challenge as well. Once a program's logic was figured out, the programmer had to go through it step by agonizing step, telling it each tiny thing to do in a binary language that had no meaning to people. Even simple programs took days to write and required the utmost concentration of experts in the anatomy of the machine.

Then, happily, the programming language arrived to save the day. It occurred to people that the coding job was really one that could best be done by the computer itself. It was, after all, the very sort of job—boring, repetitious, tedious—that the computer was built to do. And if a computer was to be used to turn human words into control codes, then there seemed to be no reason why the program could not be made a part of every computer's fund of knowledge. And that is just what was done.

Such programs are called *compilers*. When instructions are input, the compiler program goes to work. It turns commands such as READ and LET into computer control codes. Some commands (for example, the plus sign) mean several operations to the computer. The compiler knows this, and associates the command with the entire sequence of events.

Compilers and similar programs that enable people to

program in human terms are used in almost every computer. They have the effect of standardizing the formats and language along certain lines, so that anyone can learn to program without too much difficulty. Vastly different machines can be made to run the same programs, too, so that the programmer need not have an intimate knowledge of the particular machine he is using.

## Program Languages

Because compilers make standard instruction formats possible, a number of program languages which can be used on almost any computer have come into use. Humans use these languages to tell the computer what to do, and how to do it. They, like those of humans, have rules of usage, words with distinct meanings, and wide differences from language to language.

Each language has a special purpose and is designed to accomplish that goal as easily and painlessly as possible for the programmer. The most common programming languages are the following:

1. COBOL (*CO*mmon *B*usiness *O*riented *L*anguage) is about as close to ordinary English as you'll find among the instruction codes. It uses commands like "ADD PAY-RAISE TO OLD-SALARY GIVING NEW-PAY." COBOL is designed to permit people with little computer knowledge to write programs. A minimal understanding of how the computer actually works is required. The programmer needs only to understand the rules of COBOL program organization, and by using those rules he can write a program which will run without modification on any computer with a COBOL compiler. The main use of COBOL is in business programming, which

usually involves a small amount of repetitive processing on a large mass of data.

2. FORTRAN (*FOR*mula *TRAN*slator) is a language designed for scientific and mathematical use. Unlike COBOL, FORTRAN uses few English words as instructions. Instead it relies on symbols somewhat like those used in mathematics. For example, the equation $V = \sqrt{P^2 + (R - 1)^2}$ would be written $V = SQRT(P**2 + (R - 1)**2)$ in FORTRAN. In this case, SQRT is the command to find the square root of the bracketed quantity following, and ** says the next number is an exponent. In FORTRAN, a programmer can write a very complex math problem with a few instructions. Generally, the kinds of problems lending themselves to FORTRAN involve a lot of processing on a very small amount of input data, which is the opposite of COBOL situations.

3. BASIC (*B*eginner's *A*ll-purpose *S*ymbolic *I*nstruction *C*ode) is a language developed for use by students who need to run a variety of problems on remote terminals. BASIC is a fairly simple language, like COBOL in requiring little insight into the secrets of computer operation. In the past few years, BASIC has become very popular as a time-sharing language outside the schoolhouse. It can be read easily by people with little or no programming experience. The program samples shown earlier in this chapter are written in BASIC. There are some strong resemblances between BASIC and FORTRAN, but BASIC is much simpler in most respects than FORTRAN. Recently, BASIC has been expanded far beyond its original limited vocabulary in versions called ADVANCED BASIC and BII. It is comfortable in either business or mathematical applications.

In addition to these, there are many other compiler lan-

guages in use: PL/1, ALGOL, AUTOCODER, EASY-
CODER, JOVIAL, etc. Some are for use in only one
manufacturer's line of machines; others are designed for
special kinds of problems, such as the editing of alphabetic text, matrix algebra, and design of electronic
circuitry.

All programming languages have two things in common: They exist for the convenience of the people who
tell the computer what to do; and they are translated by
compilers into computer language before processing.

No matter which language he selects, the programmer
must always keep in mind that he is directing an idiot.
And although the idiot might be so accurate that a mistake in anything it undertakes is nearly impossible, and
so fast that the human mind cannot comprehend its
speed, it is still an idiot. It does not think on its own. It
only responds to commands given to it by its human
supervisors. It cannot add unless it is first told to "pick
up the pencil," and then to "put the pencil to paper." A
program language is merely a means of communication
mutually understandable to director and idiot.

# 11

# Anatomy at Work

NOW THAT YOU ARE an authority on the anatomy and direction of the computer, let's talk about some ways in which this marvelous machine serves Man.

Business data processing is the bread and butter of the computer industry. Businesses use all sorts of computers for every imaginable kind of job, but the term business data processing most often describes *batch processing* operations. We have already seen several examples of batch processing: payroll operations, billing and other jobs involving repetitive data contained on punched cards and mag tape. Often the computer assigned to this type of processing has no remote terminals. Instead, it devotes all its efforts to in-the-room jobs of a routine nature. Computer sizes range from small to gigantic, depending upon the magnitude of the business and the uses to which the machine is put. Most firms owning a computer depend on it to a great and almost overwhelming extent to perform clerical jobs. For example, a manufacturing company with combined factory and offices will have its computer record daily shipments, prepare invoices and

135

bills, process payments received, post the accounting records, balance the books of the company, and prepare reports of activities for the management. It may also be used to keep track of the inventory of parts and finished products, schedule production each day, and tell the buyers what to reorder so that the factory never runs out of supplies. It prepares the employee payroll and prints the paychecks, at the same time creating tax records for individuals and for the company. In some companies, the computer also analyzes the market for products and recommends possible new customers.

Probably more computers are used in this way than for all other purposes combined. Almost every company employing more than a thousand people has a computer of some sort at work as a business processor, and the cost and speed of computers are making it possible for much smaller firms to put them to work.

*Time-sharing* is fairly new and very fast-growing. It takes its name from the fact that a number of terminals can share the CPU at one time. Terminals, as you know, are much slower than computers. This speed differential is exploited in time-sharing. As a terminal slowly inputs data, the computer works on other terminals' jobs, pausing now and then to dump the buffer. When the input is all received, the computer runs the program in a few brief sessions, interrupting occasionally to dump other buffers, then it begins to output. Since the output is as slow as the input, the computer can run jobs for still other terminals as it pumps the results out over the line. At the same moment, it may be receiving new input from half a dozen terminals, processing several jobs, and sending output to ten other remote stations. In this way, the CPU services many terminals at once—sometimes more than a hundred—while appearing to focus all its attention on each one exclusively.

Time-sharing is very popular because it enables many people to share the costs and services of a single computer. Small businesses such as stores, doctors' offices, and repair services can have the benefits of data processing without the expense of their own computer (which they couldn't possibly afford). Likewise engineers, executives, and others who need to have problems worked out by the computer can do so cheaply, with a terminal located right beside the desk.

Many large businesses have their own time-sharing computer. Sometimes this is the same machine that does the batch work, and sometimes it is a separate machine. In some cases, the company may sell time to others outside the business to help pay for the computer. There are a number of firms whose only business is time-sharing.

*On-line systems* are similar to time-sharing, because many terminals have access to the CPU at one time. However, an on-line system is set up for a specific purpose, and it does things which a time-sharing system cannot do.

An outstanding on-line example is an airlines reservation system. The Snazzy Airline Company, let's say, has six large reservations offices all over the United States. People call the nearest office to set up their travel arrangements. Each agent has a CRT connected by a full-time phone line to the main computer in Gobbler's Knob, Nebraska. I, a future passenger, call you, an agent in the "res" office. You find out that I want to go from Stumpy Field International Airport to Whistling Fish, Maine. By keying in a few characters, you call up schedules of flights with available seats between these two major

points. These are displayed on your CRT and you read
them off to me. After I make my selection you key in my
name, address, the flight number, and certain other information, including where and when I want to pick up my
tickets. All this is input to the computer when we hang
up.

You and I think nothing more about it, but the computer's job has just begun. First it updates the passenger
list for my flight and subtracts my seat from those remaining. If my seat was the last, it strikes the flight from
the list of those with available seats. The entire record of
my reservation is stored in auxiliary memory. On the day
I want to pick up my tickets, the computer automatically
calls the location—say, a travel agency—and types out
the tickets on a terminal. A few hours before flight time,
it gets busy calling other terminals. It tells the flight line
how much fuel to put in the plane, how much luggage the
baggage people can expect, and how many meals the
kitchen should prepare. The boarding gate is provided
with a computer printout of all passengers holding reservations. All this is done automatically by the computer
under the control of its on-line programs.

This is but one on-line system, for one job. There are
many on-line systems in use today, doing everything
from running farms to tracking aircraft. The on-line system is the ultimate in computer usage.

Educators are beginning to see a great potential in
computers as "teachers." It seems a rather peculiar twist
that the idiot machine should become the teacher of the
human (rather a case of the tail wagging the dog, isn't
it?), and yet in some ways it is perfect for the job.

Take, for instance, drills in mathematics. The computer presents a problem and the student enters the answer. If the answer is correct, the student is immediately

told the good news. If not, the computer can show the student where he made his mistake. Exercises in grammar, vocabulary, history, science, and any other field of study can be taught to the computer, which then drills the student. This allows the student to progress at his own rate, being tested and receiving grades as he goes along. The grades would always be accurate, too; can you imagine anyone being called a "computer's pet"?

This is not to say that teachers are becoming less important and will eventually be done away with ("replaced by a machine"). Plain old classroom instruction is still hard to beat. Its weakness, though, is that no teacher has enough time to spend with all his or her students on drills, which is where the lessons are really learned. The teaching machine, on the other hand, has nothing else to do, no other reason to exist, but to drill students.

There are other benefits, too. If a student continues to have trouble with division but not with the other members of the math family, the computer can spot this and tip off the teacher. Then he or she can work with the student on that single trouble area and help him overcome it.

More and more adults are going back to school in their spare time, trying to keep up with the dizzying speed of technological advance. The subjects that interest adults—data processing, corporate finance, child psychology, solid-state electronics, and so on—have never been over-burdened with qualified teachers. Adult education demands have all but exhausted the supply of instructors and created a shortage of classrooms. This is going to get worse as even more people are forced by their fear of becoming outdated to continue or resume their education. Computer-aided instruction is a beautiful answer to the adult hunger for more knowledge. Using low-cost terminals in their homes and with a human teacher as close as the telephone, people will someday soon be able to take courses in anything from ancient history to astrophysics, taught by a computer, without ever leaving the living room.


Several large food store chains are moving toward the computerized supermarket. Concerned about the lines at checkout counters and the errors that cashiers, like any humans, are bound to make, these companies have put the computer to work. Every item in the store is tagged with a sticker bearing a code number that signifies the brand, size, type of product, and price. When customers bring their purchases to the checkout counter, the cashier passes these labels over an optical scanner attached via a data communications link to a central computer. As the computer reads the tags, it displays the price on a screen and rings up the amount on the cash register. When the sale is completed, the cashier operates a key, and the bill is totaled.

This system reduces errors and thus customer complaints. It also brings speedier service, since the clerks can bag the groceries while the computer goes about the process of ringing up the sale. As an added benefit to the company, the computer can update the inventory records of the store automatically, telling buyers when to reorder, analyzing customer preferences for certain brands, and detecting theft trends.

The executives of the food chains are enthusiastic about the system, and it seems certain that computerized checkout will become familiar to us all in the next few years.

We have said more than once that the uses of computers are limited only by the imaginations of people. A good example of this imagination is the Urban Traffic Control System in Washington, D.C. Transportation planners have long recognized that Washington has one of the worst traffic problems in the nation. (I can attest to that, because I work there.) Some solutions—a new subway system, more freeways, converting main arteries into one-way streets during rush hours—are either on the way to reality or already there, but they won't solve the whole problem, and everyone has known that all along.

One of the measures designed to ease the traffic problem is the Urban Traffic Control System. Every intersection in the downtown area has been equipped with weight-sensitive trips buried in the streets approaching the corners. A bank of computers working together monitor these sensors. Using average figures for the number of occupants in cars and busses and the ability to detect which and how many are in each block, the computers figure out how many people are approaching each corner. Based on these calculations the computers control the traffic lights to keep the greatest number of people moving with the smoothest efficiency. The results: fewer traffic jams, less noise from the horns of frustrated motorists, and less air pollution because masses of cars aren't standing still, belching gas fumes and going nowhere.

# 12

# Who's the Boss?

EVER SINCE THE MID-1950s, when it became possible to own and use computers on a large scale, they have had the reputation of being replacements for people.

Managers with too little concern for people and too much concern for the Mighty Corporate Dollar (happily there aren't too many of these monsters around) saw the computer as a gift from the god who creates profits. If you install a computer, they reasoned, then it can do all the work and you can fire all the people. And some did just that.

From the late 1950s to the middle 1960s, when computers had become very dependable and skillful at doing anything they were told, this became a serious national problem. It was called *automation:* to some a swearword, to others a prayer. The ownership of a computer, or perhaps several, was necessary to any self-respecting corporation. If you didn't have one, you weren't "with it." So everyone bought one, and then, frightened by the cost and drunk with the power it gave, they put it to work.

At first it hit the bookkeepers and clerks, whose routine office jobs were assumed by the computer. Some

142

people adapted by becoming programmers, operators, or keypunch workers. But plenty simply lost their jobs. Then the computer snaked its long wiry arms out into the factory, taking over machines with its process control programs. This is where it did the most damage. Assembly lines that once kept twenty or thirty people in work now needed only two or three. The others—fathers, mothers, people with families, long-term faithful employees—were fired.

As a further step in this horror story, a discovery was made: People take up space, so if you remove the people, you can put in more automated machinery. Buildings cost money to erect and even more money to maintain. It wasn't long before companies began shutting down entire plants and centralizing everything in one factory. Whole towns full of people who had always depended upon "the plant" for their living were suddenly out of work. And even worse, out of hope.

This was automation and corporate management at its uncaring worst. Happily, it didn't last too long, although certainly it was too long for the millions who went hungry because of it. The late 1960s saw fits of conscience on the part of business and society, which had allowed this to happen. Corporations became more aware of their responsibilities to employees. That doesn't mean that automation ended; but it was changed. Programs were set up by government and business to retrain persons whose jobs had been taken by the computer, and firms found gentler ways of moving employees to other jobs. Even today the social problem of automation isn't solved, but at least it is recognized and some progress is being made to overcome it.

The whole automation experience has raised an interesting and scary question: Just who's the boss?

The technological boom caused at least in part by the computer has produced some disturbing previews of the future: *1984,* by George Orwell; *Brave New World,* by Aldous Huxley; Ayn Rand's *Anthem;* and *This Perfect Day,* by Ira Levin. All four are admittedly works of fiction and fantasy, yet none are impossible, and there are some indications that we may be moving toward the dehumanized, supercontrolled, computer-dominated world they foresee.

Nearly everything of importance about almost every person in the United States is on a computer file somewhere. Department store computers keep track of what people purchase and analyze the buying habits of individual customers. Credit bureau computers know how much every adult owes, to whom, and how well they repay their debts. School computers record students' courses and grades, and never forget them. Hospital and medical research computers swallow patients' records and impersonally consider the most intimately personal workings of the human body. The computers at the U.S. Internal Revenue Service keep track of taxpayers' histories, and at the Census Bureau they even know how many toilets are in your house. The law enforcement agencies have a huge national computer system that can find within minutes the police records on any citizen.

A few years ago the Federal Government began to study the idea of creating a national data bank. All the information on every single person that is now scattered hither and yon would be brought together in this center. The purpose, it was said, was to make it easier to gather statistics. Questions such as "How many people between 18 and 21 are in college?" could be quickly answered.

No doubt this vast storehouse of information would be useful to the government. However, it smacks of *1984* and makes the admonition that "Big Brother is watching" a reality. Everything you do that creates a record—and that is almost everything of any importance—would be duly noted by this immense Peeping Tom and stored away, never to be forgotten.

To have information about a person is to wield power over him. Consider a simple example: A brother and sister are having an argument. Says the sister, "You'd better do what I want you to, or I'll tell Mom you broke that big vase in the hall." That is power in a small way (though it may not seem so small to the brother). For the government to know everything about everyone is power in a huge and frightening way. If some official were to decide to use this information to his own personal advantage, there would be no way to stop him.

Again, as in the case of automation, the tale has a happy ending. Sufficiently alarmed cries were raised over this notion that the government appears to have abandoned the project. Perhaps it really hasn't given up, but instead has buried it under the camouflage of secrecy. Even so, there's cause for relief. It hardly seems possible that the government could collect all the information about every person in every computer without attracting attention. As evidence of this, consider the great public and Congressional outcry in 1975 that resulted from revelations of the surveillance of citizens by the FBI and CIA.

Maybe we people are winning. We will remain the boss, instead of becoming bossed by the very machine we created as a tool to help us.

Business managers, as we said earlier, tend to look upon the computer as the answer to all problems. While the use of a computer as a weapon against workers has declined, it is a sad fact that the mistaken impression of

computers as error-proof machines lingers on. Most managers have only the vaguest idea of how a computer
works. They know that it costs a lot of money—a million
dollars or more—and that its caretakers use strange words
(for which the managers seldom seek definitions out of
fear of appearing ignorant) and that it does wonderful
things. Beyond that, the computer is a mystery to them.
They seem to have a sort of religious belief in it, reasoning that anything that fast, complex, and expensive *has* to
be right.

This blind faith has given birth to a new kind of crook:
the electronic thief. Since most executives accept without
question anything the computer says, programmers and
data processing people find it very simple to rob their employer. All it takes is a little cleverness with a program,
and the robber can get rich with little danger of being
caught.

One who did both (got rich *and* caught) was a programmer who had the computer write checks to people
who didn't exist. The computer sent them to his home via
the mail, and it was little trouble and well worth the effort to cash them. He got away with over $80,000 before
he was discovered.

Another way of stealing is simply to lie to the computer. Some retail store computer systems keep track of
items in the warehouse. These inventory records can be
adjusted for breakage, which is a fact of life where large
amounts of merchandise arc stored. A computer operator
can easily enter a false breakage report on, say, a color
television set, then carry the set off in his car. If he is really cautious, he can even create a false receipt of sale,
which he never inputs to the computer.

There is always a danger in payroll processing. The
computer people get paid by the same system as everyone

else, of course, but they have the advantage of setting up and running the system. It is little trouble for a programmer to create a false employee in the tape file and take the paycheck for himself. Another way is to subtract a penny from everyone's wages and have the computer write him a check for the total, perhaps even in the course of running some other program later on.

It is not just the unquestioning managers who make electronic theft easy. A skillful thief can pull off a holdup in a whole room full of programmers and never be noticed. It is possible to write an honest program that runs perfectly every time, but that can be changed to a crooked one by altering one instruction. Often last-minute changes are made before a program run. The programmer can insert his "stick-up" instruction, which by itself looks as innocent as a ceiling, and no one will think a thing about it.

Robbery is a serious crime that everyone wants controlled. But electronic thieves are smart and they have the advantage of knowing their machines and programs better than anyone else. This makes it difficult, if not impossible, to catch them. I wish I could tell you that this story, like the others in this chapter, has a happy ending, but I cannot. No one knows how much electronic stealing is going on, but some experts predict that one of these days a swindle worth hundreds of millions of dollars will be discovered.

The computer is a tool invented by Man to serve Man. So is a train. But if the train runs away, it takes all its passengers helplessly along with it. In that case, who's the boss?

This is about what has happened with the computer. In the 1950s no one could foresee the enormous speed-up of progress that the computer would bring. Most businesses bought them because they could do more work faster than people, and at less cost. That is still true. The nature of Man does not change, and computers are getting better. The computer will always be better at some jobs than we are, and that is why it is so successful. The purpose of any tool we create is to make up for shortcomings we have. In this case, the tool makes up for slowness and inaccuracy.

We have not always recognized these as shortcomings. Back in the days when a horse's gait was the measure of travel over land and a ship could never hope to move faster than the wind, the leisurely pace of the human was enough. Life went on in a deliberate sort of way, with now and then a thinker creating some new tool to overcome a specific example of slowness: the printing press, the cotton gin, the automatic loom. But slowness as a characteristic of the human species was not recognized.

Inaccuracy was, and some thought went into means of overcoming it. The abacus, a sort of "adding machine," was invented thousands of years ago. The ancient Greeks, we have learned from archaeology, had a crude calculating machine. Charles Babbage, a British mathematician, developed plans in the early 1800s for two mechanical computers. His machines were designed to eliminate the rampant human errors in numerical tables. All of these devices are evidence that inaccuracy has been a serious concern all along. With few exceptions, though, no one believed that anything could be done about it.

And anyway, Man was doing all right despite his bumbling, erring ways. Some improvements—the Industrial Revolution, for instance—caused trouble and made everyone squirm a little, but in the long run we recovered and life was made a little nicer at each step. In troubled times, one could look back and take comfort in this experience; and any big stride was always followed by a time of quiet, when everyone could adjust to it.

Then came the computer, and the train ran away. Suddenly we became painfully aware that we are pokey and sloppy. This single machine could finish more in a few minutes than a whole brigade of wizards could begin in a year. The moment we perceived the tremendous power of this machine, we began to find ways to use it.

Scientists who formerly required years, whole lifetimes even, to devise and prove theories could now do so in hours or days. Businessmen, doctors, engineers, economists, researchers, students, sociologists, and anybody else could get answers to any questions they chose to ask in a fraction of the time it used to take.

The knowledge curve swung sharply upward. In George Washington's day, the total of all knowledge was doubling perhaps every hundred years or so. The more you know, the greater the base upon which you can build and the faster you can learn yet more. Thus, by the middle of this century, when the computer emerged from the laboratory, Man was doubling what he knew every twenty-five years. Now, with the computer about a quarter of a century old, the sum of knowledge is said to double every three years. Four and a half years from now, it will have doubled twice over today's. At that rate, in six years we will be doubling what we already know *every single day!*

But wait! Just how much can we take? How much new knowledge can mankind swallow? You can only pump a certain amount of water down a pipe at one time, no matter how much pressure you exert. Grandma knew she could only force-feed the Christmas goose so much before it literally exploded and died. When are we going to reach the point where we simply can't keep up anymore?

No one knows. We are creatures who evolved slowly, in our own good time. Since civilization began, we have evolved and developed largely under our own control, at our own rate of speed. But now, like the passengers on the train, we have lost some of that control and let the tool we created for our own convenience run away with us.

Where will it stop, or at least get back under control? The question cannot be answered because we have never faced such a crisis before, and thus we have no experience upon which to base a prediction.

Maybe we, as our ancestors used to do, can "look back and take comfort" in past experience. Perhaps this is just another troubled time, like the Industrial Revolution, which will be followed by a quiet period when we can catch up with ourselves.

Maybe.

One thing is certain. The computer is here to stay. Every day and in every way, its tiny pulses of massive power are becoming more of an indispensable organ of humanity. Already the influence of this machine touches the lives of every person in the civilized world. As the importance of the computer grows, which it is certain to do, more and more people will be compelled to familiarize themselves with this magical idiot.

It falls to all of us to make certain that this powerful tool we have created for our convenience continues to be used for our good.

# Appendix A

HERE IS a review and some exercises in binary math.

*Addition* deserves only a review here, since it was pretty thoroughly covered in Chapter 4. The rules, as you'll recall, are:

$$0 + 0 = 0$$
$$0 + 1 = 1$$
$$1 + 0 = 1$$
$$1 + 1 = 0 \text{ with a carry of } 1$$

Examples:
1. Add 2 and 6.

$$
\begin{array}{r}
\mathbf{11} \\
0010 \\
+\,0110 \\
\hline
1000
\end{array}
\qquad
\begin{array}{r}
2 \\
+\,6 \\
\hline
8
\end{array}
$$

2. Add 9 and 6 using BCD digits (use complementing to handle the overflow).

```
    1001              9
  + 0110            + 6
```
```
    1111                  15 (overflow)
  + 0101     (complement of 1010, overflow adjust-
                 ment)
```
```
  10100     (sum of false 15 plus 10 complement)
      1     (end-around carry)
```
```
0001   0101   Real answer in BCD
```

*Subtraction* can take one of two routes. The most common in computers is the complementing method. Here we take the number being subtracted from another number (the subtrahend) and change each bit to its opposite. For instance, 1001 becomes 0110. Then we add it to the minuend. The sum is always one bit longer than the numbers we are adding, so we take the left bit off and add it to the right bit. This is end-around carry, and it yields the answer. Like this:

Subtract 4 from 6 using complementing.

```
  111
  0110
+ 1011     (complement of 0100, binary 4)
```
```
10001
    1     (end-around carry)
```
```
 0010     The answer, binary 2
```

Complementing is a long and laborious method for us people. For the computer, it is easier and that is why it's used. The opposite holds true, then. Our "easy method" is complicated for the computer.

These are the rules of true binary subtraction:

$$0 - 0 = 0$$
$$1 - 1 = 0$$
$$1 - 0 = 1$$
$$0 - 1 = 1 \text{ with a borrow from the next column.}$$

There is more to that borrowing rule than we had room for in the table of laws, so let's discuss it here. The borrow has to be from a higher-order 1. You can't borrow 1 from nothing, so if the top of the next column contains a 1 you borrow it by changing it to 0 and following the rule from there, but if it's a 0 you have to go hunting for a 1. You change the 0 to 1, then move another column to the left and change that bit to its complement. If it's a 1, the borrow is satisfied and you return to the place where you started and bring down a 1 to the answer. If it is a 0, however, you have to keep working to the left until you finally find a 1.

That's a lot of words. Let's look at some examples.

1. Subtract 5 from 6 using true binary subtraction.

$$\begin{array}{cc} \mathbf{0} & \\ 01\cancel{1}0 & 6 \\ -\,0101 & -\,5 \\ \hline 0001 & 1 \end{array}$$

2. Subtract 3 from 4.

$$\begin{array}{cc} \mathbf{01} & \\ 0\cancel{1}\cancel{0}0 & 4 \\ -\,0011 & -\,3 \\ \hline 0001 & 1 \end{array}$$

3. Subtract 1 from 8.

$$\begin{array}{cc} \mathbf{011} & \\ \cancel{1}\cancel{0}\cancel{0}0 & 8 \\ -\,0001 & -\,1 \\ \hline 0111 & 7 \end{array}$$

While on paper the process of subtraction appears simpler than complementary addition, it is considerably more complex in electronic registers. The task of seeking a 1 in the minuend and complementing portions (individual bits) of a BCD digit requires a lot of circuitry and manipulation of the bit string. For this reason, complementing is preferred.

*Multiplication* really begins to give us insight into the computer makers' preference for multiple addition. The rules of binary multiplication are:

1. If the multiplier bit is a 1, copy the entire multiplicand; if the multiplier bit is a 0, bring down only a 0.
2. Shift as in decimal multiplication.
3. Add the binary numbers (subproducts) according to the rules of addition.

Since our concern here is with BCD numbers, these rules should be amended with another which will make the process simpler: Keep a running subtotal of the subproducts during the multiplication, and adjust for overflow whenever necessary. Examples:

1. Multiply 3 by 2.

| | | |
|---|---|---|
| 0011 | | 3 |
| × 0010 | | × 2 |
| 0 | 1st shift subproduct | |
| 0011 | 2nd shift " | |
| 00110 | Subtotal | |
| 0 | 3rd shift " | |
| 00110 | Subtotal | |
| 0 | 4th shift " | |
| 00110 | Total product | 6 |

2. Multiply 5 by 3.

```
        0101                                         5
      × 0011                                       × 3

        0101    1st shift subproduct
        0101    2nd shift        ″

        01111   Subtotal
       −1010    Adjustment for overflow
0001    0101    BCD subtotal
        0       3rd shift subproduct

0001    0101    Subtotal
        0       4th shift subproduct

0001    0101    BCD product                         15
```

3. Multiply 7 by 5.

```
        0111                                         7
      × 0101                                       × 5

        0111    1st shift subproduct
        0       2nd shift        ″

        0111    Subtotal
        0111    3rd shift        ″

        100011  Subtotal
       −001010  Adjustment for overflow
 0001   11001   Subtotal
+0001   −1010   Adjustment for overflow

 0010   1111    Subtotal
+0001   −1010   Adjustment for overflow

 0011   0101    Subtotal
        0       4th shift subproduct

 0011   0101    Total product                       35
```

As you can see, the water begins to get pretty muddy when you have to cope with an overflow. In the third example, three adjustments were necessary before the overflow subproduct was reduced to a workable number. Another problem in binary multiplication is the number of possible bits that can come out of a single operation. Eighty-one is the highest possible product ($9 \times 9 = 81$), and it is a seven-bit character: 1010001. So a multiplication register would need to store up to seven bits, which makes it an expensive piece of circuitry. It is a lot easier from the design viewpoint to do multiple addition.

*Division,* too, is quite complicated in its true form, which again bears out the wisdom of the folks who bring you the add-only arithmetic unit. The rules are:

1. Delete all high-order (left-hand) 0's; for instance 0011 becomes 11.
2. Start from the left of the dividend, as in long division.
3. Shifting right at each step, perform a series of subtractions in which the divisor is subtracted from the dividend.
4. If subtraction is possible (minuend greater than subtrahend), subtract and place a 1 in the quotient.
5. If subtraction is not possible (minuend smaller than subtrahend), put a 0 in the quotient. Then bring down the next bit from the dividend to the right-hand end of the set from which subtraction was not possible.

Let's do a few examples to see how these rules work.
1. Divide 6 by 2.

$$6 = 0110 = 110$$
$$2 = 0010 = 10$$

$$\begin{array}{r} 11 = 0011 = 3 \text{ (the answer)} \\ 10\,\overline{)110} \end{array}$$

| | |
|---|---|
| 10 | Subtraction possible; 1 to quotient |
| 10 | Difference and 0 from dividend brought down. |
| 10 | Subtraction possible; 1 to quotient. |

2. Divide 8 by 2.

$8 = 1000$
$2 = 0010 = 10$

$$100 = 0100 = 4 \text{ (the answer)}$$

$$10\overline{)1000}$$

| | |
|---|---|
| 10 | Subtraction possible; 1 to quotient. |
| 00 | Difference and 0 from dividend brought down. |
| 10 | Subtr. not possible; 0 to quotient. |
| 00 | 0 brought down to same set. |
| 10 | Subtr. not possible; 0 to quotient. |

3. Divide 27 by 3. This problem involves an added step in which we convert the two-digit number 27 (0010 0111) into a single stream of bits meaning 27.

$3 = 0011 = 11$
$27 = 0010\ 0111$(to convert, subtract 1 from the tens and add ten to the units, repeating until the tens $= 0000$).

```
  0010        0111
– 0001     +  1010
 ──────    ────────
  0001       10001
– 0001     +  1010
 ──────    ────────
  0000       11011
```

11011 is the dividend. It has a value of 27, which you can prove by computing its place values.

Now to divide:

$$1001 = 9 \text{ (the answer)}$$

$11\,\overline{)\overline{11011}}$

| $\underline{11}$ | Subtraction possible; 1 to quotient. |
| 00 | Difference and 0 from dividend brought down. |
| $\underline{11}$ | Subtr. not possible; 0 to quotient. |
| 01 | 1 brought down to same set. |
| $\underline{11}$ | Subtr. not possible; 0 to quotient. |
| 11 | 1 brought down to same set. |
| $\underline{11}$ | Subtraction possible; 1 to quotient. |

Once again we see why this method has never achieved great popularity among the computer makers. Think of the conversion to change 18529 into a divisible number! Then to store it, you would need a fifteen-bit register, since it would be written 100100001100001. In fact, you would need registers of an infinite length, since computers work in numbers much, much greater than the mere 18529. This becomes impractical in any but very specialized computers; thus the multiple subtraction method carries the field.

We promised you some problems to work in BCD. None are very difficult—it's doubtful you will ever be called upon to work quadratic equations in binary—because the intent is not to challenge you, but rather to broaden your understanding of the binary system. In the jargon of the computer world, this is called "hands-on" experience.

In Chapter 4 and again in this appendix we have looked at several methods of computation. It matters not whether you use the short or long methods, complementing or true forms. Whichever you choose, the answers should come out the same. If they don't, I suggest you lay the blame with the mathematician and not with the methods. This book contains all the rules and examples you will need to work the exercises. If your brow gets wrinkled and your scalp begins to hurt from too much scratching over a problem that simply won't come out, try another method or else review the examples.

These problems show the answers without divulging the methods. Some writers like to hide the answers upside down elsewhere in the book. I don't believe in that, since the important thing is not to find the answer itself, but to *learn how* to find it.

This is not a test. We won't tell a soul how you did. Relax and have fun being a human binary computer.

| 1. | | 2. | | 3. | | 4. | |
|---|---|---|---|---|---|---|---|
| | 0011 | | 0011 | | 0011 | | 0110 |
| | + 0010 | | − 0010 | | × 0010 | | ÷ 0011 |
| | 0101 | | 0001 | | 0110 | | 0010 |

| 5. | | 6. | | 7. | |
|---|---|---|---|---|---|
| | 0010 | | 0010 | | 0001 0001 |
| | × 0110 | | + 1001 | | − 0000 0111 |
| | 0001 0010 | | 0001 0001 | | 0000 0100 |

| 8. | | 9. | | 10. | |
|---|---|---|---|---|---|
| | 0001 0010 | | 1001 | | 1001 |
| | ÷ 0000 0110 | | + 1001 | | − 1001 |
| | 0000 0010 | | 0001 1000 | | 0000 |

| 11. | | 12. | | 13. | |
|---|---|---|---|---|---|
| | 0001 1000 | | 0001 0010 | | 0001 0001 |
| | ÷ 0000 0011 | | × 0000 0010 | | + 0000 0010.0101 |
| | 0000 0110 | | 0010 0100 | | 0001 0011.0101 |

| 14. | | 15. | | 16. | |
|---|---|---|---|---|---|
| | 0010.0101 | | 0111 | | 0100 1000 |
| | × 0000 0010 | | × 0111 | | ÷ 0000 0110 |
| | 0000 0101 | | 0100 1001 | | 0000 1000 |

17.  0001 1001
    − 0001 0000
    ──────────
           1001

18.  0001 0011
    × 0000 0011
    ──────────
     0011 1001

19.  0001 0111
    − 0001 0001
    ──────────
     0000 0110

20.  1001
    ÷ 0010
    ──────────
     0100.0101

21.      0101 0001
       + 0110 0011
       ──────────
     0001 0000 0100

22.  0111
    + 0011
    ──────
    − 0010
    ──────
      1000

23.  0001 0101 0000
    ÷ 0000 0101 0000
    ──────────────
     0000 0000 0011

24.      0001 0001
       × 0001 0001
       ──────────
     0001 0010 0001

25.  0001 0110
    + 0000 1001
    + 0010 0001
    ──────────
     0100 0110

26.  0010 0011.1001 0100
    − 0000 0110.1001 0101
    ──────────────────
     0001 0110.1001 1001

27.  0010 0100.0010
    × 0000 0000.0010
    ──────────────
     0100 1000.0100

28.              0100 0111
               ÷ 0000 0100
        ──────────────────
     0001 0001.0111 0101

29.  0001 0001 0011
    + 0000 1001 0110
    + 0000 0001 0100
    ──────────────
     0010 0010 0011

30.        0100
          × 0100
          × 0100
        ────────
     0110 0100

31.  1001 0001
    − 1000 0010
    ──────────
     0000 1001

32.  0001 0001 0000
    ÷ 0000 0000 0101
    ──────────────
     0000 0000 0101

33.      0001 0101
       × 0001 0101
     ────────────
     0010 0010 0101

34.    1001
      × 0011
     ────────
     0010 0111

35.    1001
      + 0011
     ────────
     0001 0010

36.  0010 0111
    − 0001 0010
    ──────────
     0001 0101

37.  0001 0101
    ÷ 0000 0011
    ──────────
     0000 0101

(Do you recognize 34 through 37 from somewhere?)

If you would like to do more exercises, here's a way:

1. Write the problem, but not the answer, in decimal.
2. Translate the decimal digits to BCD.
3. Work the problem and find the answer in BCD.
4. Translate the BCD numbers into decimal.
5. Work the problem in decimal, and compare the answers.

# Appendix B

## Computer Careers

I DON'T know if it is possible to dedicate a piece of a book to someone, but if it is, this appendix is dedicated to those considering a career in computer.

Because of the explosive growth in computer importance and effect, it is hard to imagine a career more filled with opportunity. Certainly the last chapter demonstrated that the computer is a permanent feature of civilization.

The successful operation of a computer requires the combined skills of many people. Even a small machine needs twenty or so people to support it. Large installations may call for as many as a couple of hundred, although the average is probably about fifty per machine. If you figure that 10,000 new computers "go on the air" each year, a bit more math will tell you that 1,350 new computer workers are needed *every day*.

That is an awfully good job market. There aren't enough qualified people to go around now, and the need is growing a lot faster than the numbers of people arriving to fill it.

As a result, the opportunities are splendid for those who are qualified. Companies with a lot of money tied up in a computer have to have the people to run the thing, so they are willing to pay handsomely in most cases to get them. Another benefit of this rapid growth is that advancement is very fast for those who have the necessary credentials. I've met very few data processing executives over forty and I know of several who haven't yet reached thirty. You will find few gray heads around a data processing center.

To emphasize a point that can't be stressed enough: qualifications are absolutely necessary! The job market may be nearing desperation, but the machinery as an investment and the role it plays in the organization and in society as a whole are too important to turn over to just anyone who chances along. Those who would get ahead in the data business *must have* both experience and education.

What sort of education? That depends on what you want to do. There will be more on this as we talk about specific jobs. The rule in general, however, is that the more education you have, the better your opportunities. As for experience, you get that by working in a data center. Some can be had in school— courses in programming, processing management, etc.—but you can't just get a degree in computer science and then take over as the boss. As someone once remarked, "You don't learn about fishing from a book; you learn about fishing from fish." So it is with data processing. My advice is, get as much schooling as you possibly can, whether it be a high school diploma or a doctorate in cybernetics, and then get a job and work hard. If you do that your career will take care of itself.

The rewards in this field go far beyond dollars and position. Computers, as you have seen, are used almost everywhere, for almost every undertaking. Business, of course, is the biggest user and thus provides the largest market in which to sell your services. Some people, though, don't care much for business and if you are one of them, don't despair. You're not locked out of the computer room at all. Politics, education, social work, research, government, medicine, racial integration, and anything else that is happening all depend in some fashion on computers. Even churches are now going into data processing. Whatever your "thing" is, you can contribute to it in a very important way through a career in computers.

A message for women: Data processing is one of the few professional fields in which women have always had total equality with men (without having to fight for it). More than one data processing executive has stated that women make better programmers and analysts than men. I don't know if this has been proven beyond all doubt, but I do know that women have been traditionally well treated in this field.

Every job has its good and its bad sides. Data processing as a career has more plusses than minuses. On the good side are the conditions: The work is interesting and varied; the surroundings are pleasant; co-workers are usually intelligent and well-informed people; and the pay is relatively high with bright prospects for advancement. The bad may not be too bad, depending upon your personal tastes: unending tiny details; bewildering problems at times, leading to frustration; hard work that often doesn't end until long after the rest of the world has gone home; occasional and sometimes crushing pressure from higher management. Even when the bad is at its worst, though, there is comfort in knowing that the work is worthwhile. And very few things in this life are more satisfying than standing back after all is done and watching that computer work its miracles just as you have told it to do.

The jobs in data processing break down into two general categories: craft and professional. Craft jobs are the lower-level starting positions. As a rule people in these jobs are paid on the basis of hours worked, so they punch a timeclock and get paid extra for overtime work. Craft people do not supervise others. Professional people, on the other hand, are managers. Depending upon their job responsibilities they may or may not have other professionals or craft people reporting to them. They don't punch a timeclock and quite frequently they get nothing extra for overtime work. Their salaries, however, are higher than craft wages. In most organizations, professional jobs are filled by promotions from the craft levels. Some are also filled by new employees with experience elsewhere or with advanced degrees from colleges. Most beginners in data processing enter the field at the craft level and then move upward. Generally the better your education, the faster you rise and the higher you get.

There is no point in listing salaries for the different positions. These vary widely by location and by employer, as well as being subject to economic conditions. The best place to find out how much employers are paying is the "help-wanted" section of the Sunday paper in the area where you would like to live. Look under computers, data, programmers, systems analysts, and other headings for the specific jobs you're interested in.

Most employers offer a number of fringe benefits that are worth money to the worker. These, too, vary quite a lot, but usually they include paid vacations, life and health insurance, a retirement pension plan, and a discount on the products or services sold by the employer. Some also have bonuses, plans for buying shares in the company at a reduced cost, assistance in paying for part-time schooling, and awards for outstanding job performance. Often, employers don't mention the fringe benefits in their help-wanted ads. However, the personnel department or employment agency posting the ad can tell you what they are, and you should ask if you are serious about applying.

What kind of education should you get in order to prepare yourself for a career in data processing? The first rule is that you must have at least a high school diploma. Beyond that, get as much as you can. One word of caution: In almost any computer room you will find one "mustang," a person with an eighth-grade education who is now a mathematical programmer, or a data processing manager whose college training amounts to one course in bible study. These people are exceptions, not the rule. Don't delude yourself into believing you will be one of them. They are a healthy sign that data processing isn't a hidebound profession like law or teaching, which requires a minimum education in special courses. They mean that anyone with ambition and desire can get ahead in the field. But *you* get as much career-oriented schooling as you can.

There are many schools of the business-college variety that offer short courses in keypunching, programming, and related subjects. Some are good and some will just take your money, so be careful. As a general rule, the more glittering their promises, the less they really deliver. This has been amply demonstrated by numerous scandals involving such schools over the past few years. A lot of technical schools and the military services now have courses in computer science and data processing. Some are strongly slanted toward repair and maintenance of computer hardware, while others focus mainly on programming and the administration of data processing. In terms of beginning jobs, graduates of these courses often are treated the same as those with college. Later, though, the holder of a four-year degree will begin to outrace the tech school graduate.

It is sometimes possible to get computer training through an employer. Some companies advertise in the papers or list computer jobs with employment agencies stating "No experience necessary" or "We will train you." You will have to take aptitude tests in addition to other more standard preemployment tests. These same companies and many others usually also offer their existing employees such training opportunities. The advantage here is that the training is paid for by your employer, and you will draw a salary while going to school. And if you fail the aptitude tests, keep trying; your score will improve with practice.

The four-year college is really the best place to prepare for any career, including data processing. You'll find programmers and managers and analysts from almost every field of study. Many majored in business administration, but there are a lot of sociologists, mathematicians, psychologists, engineers, and linguists in data processing, too. A programmer has to be an expert in the subject his programs deal with, so if you want to be in data processing in a chemical research industry, you would do well to study chemistry and related sciences in college. If you have no specialized interests, then "generalize" in a business or liberal arts major, perhaps going a bit heavy on math and accounting. Nearly all colleges offer a series of courses in data processing and programming. Take at least a few of them, and preferably all of them.

There are also graduate courses leading to advanced degrees in various fields within data processing; mathematical statistics and operations research are a couple of examples. They're great if you can handle them academically and financially, because they nearly guarantee your success.

Computer work requires some aptitudes. You have to be patient and methodical; there is no room for emotions and frustration in this business. You must have a sense of mechanics and the ability to grasp large and abstract problems easily, breaking them down into a logical step-by-step sequence. It helps to be able to get along well with others, because the nature of the work will place you in a cooperative, teamwork situation. Above all, you need an inquiring mind that never tires of new challenges and is never satisfied with "good enough."

What kinds of jobs are there? I've grouped the positions into several categories. This is by no means a complete itemization, but rather a general listing of the sorts of things you'll find people doing in nearly every fair-sized computer room.

1. Keypunch operator (craft). Punches cards and prepares other input from source documents. Verifies the accuracy of cards. Promotion to keypunch supervisor, librarian, or coder. Education: high school.

2. Librarian (craft). Maintains library of mag tapes, card decks, disk packs, etc. Also takes care of books, brochures, and manuals used by computer people. Promotion to chief librarian or computer operator. Education: high school.

3. Coder (craft). Translates program flowcharts into input language such as COBOL or FORTRAN. Works closely with programmers. Promotion to programmer, sometimes computer operator. Education: high school or tech school. College graduates occasionally start here too.

4. Computer operator (usually craft). Runs the computer; inputs cards, mounts and dismounts tapes, etc. Often helps programmers debug, troubleshoots machine problems. The operator has to know the computer better than anyone else. Advancement to programmer, assistant data processing manager, or chief operator.

5. Programmer. This is a very broad category. Programmers convert plans and objectives into computer procedures. There are many kinds of programmers:

a. Junior programmer (craft). Beginners start here. Close work with senior programmers developing sections of programs. Rapid promotion to senior programmer (often six months to a year). Education: high school if promoted to the job; tech school or college if starting.

b. General programmer (professional). Develops a wide range of business programs, usually of a repetitive nature such as payroll and accounting routines. Supervises codes and junior programmers. Promotion to systems analyst or data processing manager. Education: tech school or college.

c. Scientific programmer (professional). Works with engineers and scientists to develop special and very technical programs. May supervise juniors and coders. Requires special knowledge of the field worked in. Often a career position, but promotion to DPM (Data Processing Manager) or outside field to engineering management is possible. Education: engineering, science or math degree. Graduate work is desirable.

d. Industrial programmer (professional). Develops process control programs to run machinery in factories. Promotion to systems analyst or outside to production department. Education: degree in industrial or mechanical engineering.

6. Systems analyst (professional). Studies operations in a business or other organization and finds ways to use data processing to improve them. Develops overall plans from which programmers and others work. Often leads to data processing manager or executive positions elsewhere in the organization. Education: college degree (business preferred) and programming experience.

7. Operations researcher (professional). Develops math models of situations. These are intricate programs that predict complex behavior. For instance, a model is devised to determine a company's change in profitability if any part of its financial structure is altered. Models predict the behavior of everything from bridge structures to the selling price of paper clips. They answer the question "What if?" Operations researchers study the subject to be modeled and reduce it to mathematical terms. Usually a career position, but it can lead to executive positions. Education: advanced degree in math or operations research plus programming experience.

8. Data processing manager (professional). The boss of the computer operations. All the occupations listed above fall under this person's control. The DPM is responsible for the computer, for the people who run it, and for the uses to which it is put. While this is the top spot, promotion to upper management (a vice presidency, for example) is possible. Education: college degree and wide experience in all aspects of data processing.

These jobs are all on the user end of the computer business: the firms and agencies which buy or rent computers and use them for their own purposes. On the other end are the computer manufacturers, whose business it is to provide the equipment and services to the users.

This area, too, is a fertile field for the career seeker. The demand for new computers is continually increasing, which means more and more people are needed to produce them. In

addition, new technology (created, ironically, by the very computers they manufacture) forces the producers to work constantly on improving their products. And as users become ever
more dependent upon their computers and gain knowledge of
their abilities (and inabilities), they place heavy demands on
computer firms for special equipment and software. It takes
people to satisfy these requirements, too.

Preparing for a career in computer manufacturing is no different than preparing for one in computer usage. All of the
same occupations exist on the producers' side, plus a few. As a
rule, the producers train their own employees more thoroughly
than the users, because (1) they are better equipped to do so,
and (2) they are expected to be represented by experts.

Many of the programmers and analysts work with customers
as consultants, assisting them with special needs. So do the engineers who design computer hardware. These people must be
very sharp in their skills. It is a fascinating and rewarding
field, being exposed to a tremendous variety of operations,
solving a whole range of problems. The pay is good, too;
usually considerably higher than the users'. But the work is
hard, the hours are long, and hotels begin to look more like
home than the place where you really live.        ·

One of the greatest needs in computer manufacturing is for
industrial, mechanical, and electrical engineers. Computer producers are themselves heavily dependent upon computerized
process control to turn out the amazingly complex, tiny circuits
used in the electronics of the systems. They constantly seek
new ways to automate their production lines, and this takes a
lot of industrial engineering talent. Mechanical and electrical
engineers are usually trained extensively in specialized areas,
such as control unit design or the refinement of reading stations
on card equipment. Again, the pay is good and such engineers
become extremely valuable because of their detailed knowledge. The only drawback is that if the equipment of specializa-
tion becomes out of date, so does the engineer. The best way

to prepare for such a career is to get a degree in the branch of engineering that interests you, then apply with the employer for a job. He will fit you in where you are needed and would be happiest.

Another area is maintenance and repair. Computers need constant loving care; they are prone to all sorts of strange ills, and even the healthiest of them has to be shut down once a week or so for routine checks. The people who do this work—the computer doctors—are usually called customer engineers, or CE's for short. Since most computers are owned by the manufacturers and rented to the users, most of the maintenance and repair is done by CE's employed by these producer-owners. CE's are often tech school graduates, many or most of them with military experience in electronics work. They really aren't engineers in the sense of those we have talked about already, but rather they are technicians who test and repair equipment. The employers train these people extensively, and for a good reason; they are the folks who make the thing work, and they had better know what they are doing before they start tearing a million-dollar machine apart. The pay is very good—CE's earn more than a lot of college graduates—but advancement is not particularly rapid. One way around this hurdle is to work as a CE and take college courses toward an engineering degree in your spare time. When you get a degree, you have a tremendous wealth of practical experience that will buy advancement.

Let's not forget the people who keep the industry going: the salesmen. One of the oldest and wisest sayings in commerce is that "nothing happens until somebody sells something." Too many people think of salesmen as the untidy fast-talkers who come unbidden to the door to pressure them into buying some outrageous gadget they couldn't possibly need. That idea couldn't be less true of computer salesmen. They seldom call unless invited. They take time and care in studying the customer's operation, and they work closely with the customer in developing his needs. As a rule, these people are well-groomed, well-paid, well-informed professionals. They don't do any fast-talking, nor do they pressure anyone. The computer salesman has to be many things: programmer, systems analyst, business expert, equipment engineer. He must know everything about his company, his product, and his customer. The typical salesman has a college degree in business administration and a year or more of training in his job. The pay is outstanding, but again, it is earned with hard work, no set hours, and travel to the point of nausea. Is it worth it? "You better believe it," says one computer salesman. "It's the best job in the world."

You could say the same about any computer career.

# Appendix C

## Glossary of Data Processing Terms

Data processing is an industry that hides much common sense behind a screen of exotic, forbidding terms. Every occupation has its jargon, its own words, and usages by which the "insider" is identified and by which aspects of the profession are described with precision by those "in the know"—although the precision is lost on the "outsider." Data processing probably has more of these terms than any other occupation.

Throughout this book, we have defined such words and uses as they emerged in the text. These definitions, however, are scattered hither and yon, making it difficult to find them. For that reason this glossary is included as a reference.

Not all the terms defined in the book will be found here. This appendix contains only the most important and frequently used words. If you don't find the one you're seeking here, check the index.

**Accumulator.** The main register in the arithmetic/logic unit.
**Adder.** An electronic circuit, the function of which is to add binary digits.
**Address.** A specific location within the computer's memory.

**Arithmetic/logic unit.** A component of the CPU in which mathematical and logical operations are performed.

**Auxiliary memory.** Low-speed mass storage under the control of the CPU and organized by addresses.

**Binary.** A numbering plan based upon two states of electricity (either on and off or plus and minus). These states are represented as the digits 1 and 0. The base of numbering in binary is two, in contrast to the base of ten in our decimal scheme.

**Bit.** A binary digit, which may be either a 1 or a 0; the smallest unit of information.

**Buffer.** A small memory which adjusts speed differences between main memory and external devices.

**Byte.** A computer character normally consisting of eight bits, in which the first four bits classify the meaning of the last four bits.

**Central Processing Unit.** The brains of the computer. Consists of control unit, arithmetic/logic unit, and main memory.

**Character.** A graphic symbol such as a letter of the alphabet; a set of bits with a fixed meaning.

**Code.** A set of characters.

**Comparison.** One of the three basic activities of the computer. The process of examining two quantities or conditions in order to determine their relationship. Results in a decision that influences subsequent action taken by the computer.

**Computer.** A high-speed electronic machine which operates on information by performing mathematical functions, making decisions as it goes along, and remembering what it must do and what it has done.

**Control unit.** A component of the CPU which controls the entire computer system.

**Conversational mode.** The ability of a computer and a terminal to exchange information.

**Core.** A type of memory system.

**Counter.** A register that counts occurrences of some condition or activity within the central processor.

**CPU.** See Central Processing Unit.

**Cybernetics.** The study of the workings of the human mind and the application of this study to computer design.

**Data.** Information in a raw form. Data is operated on in order to solve problems and produce results.

**Data communications.** The movement of information by electronic means.

**Data processing.** A series of planned activities in which raw information is reworked in order to produce new and meaningful information, usually involving a computer.

**Data set.** An electronic device which conditions signals so that they may be sent over communications media.

**Electronics.** The use of electricity to convey information.

**Executive program.** The basic set of instructions telling the computer how to perform its functions.

**Field.** A portion of a data record.

**Flowchart.** A pictorial diagram of the logic of a program.

**Format.** The order in which input and output are arranged.

**Hardware.** The machinery comprising a computer system. Contrasts with software.

**Input.** Programs and data entered into the computer; a device which reads media; the act of entering such information.

**Keypunch.** A machine which produces punched cards for computer input by operation of a keyboard similar to that of a typewriter. When used as a verb, to operate such a machine.

**Logic.** Reasoning and acting upon the decisions made while reasoning.

**Logic circuit.** An electronic device that performs some intelligent job, e.g., an adder.

**Logic unit.** See arithmetic/logic unit.

**Medium.** A carrier of information, such as a punched card or air when carrying sound waves (plural is *media*).

**Memory.** One of the three basic characteristics of the computer. The portion of the computer that remembers data and programs.

**Modem.** See "data set."

**Operations research.** A branch of computer science dealing with the creation of mathematical models to simulate real-life conditions. These models are used to answer questions beginning with "What if?" For instance, if a marketing executive asks, "What if we advertise our coffins in physical fitness magazines?" a model can predict the potential added business for each dollar spent on the ads.

**Overflow.** The condition in which a computer encounters a situation outside predefined limits.

**Output.** The results of data processing. Output may either be in a graphic form (words, drawings, displays) or in the form of action (process control, for instance). Also, a device which permits output.

**Process control.** Computer control of complex machinery, usually but not always in a factory.

**Processing.** See data processing.

**Processor.** A computer.

**Program.** A set of precise instructions that a computer follows in working out problems.

**Real-time.** A type of computer system in which the processor acts upon input and returns the results immediately.

**Register.** A temporary storage device associated with logic circuitry.

**Results.** The product of data processing.

**Software.** The procedures and programs used to make a computer system work. This includes as its main feature the executive program. Contrasts with hardware.

**Storage.** See memory.

**System.** A group of elements working together as a complete unit in order to accomplish a task. A computer system encompasses both hardware and software.

**Terminal.** A machine which communicates with a computer from a distance, via data communications.

**Turnaround document.** An output medium which is sent out of the computer room and later returned to be used as an input medium.

**Word.** A group of bytes or characters handled as a unit of information by the computer.

# For Further Reading

AWAD, ELIAS M., and the Data Processing Management Association. *Automatic Data Processing: Principles and Procedures,* Prentice-Hall, Englewood Cliffs, N.J., 1966.

BARTEE, THOMAS C. *Digital Computer Fundamentals, Second Edition,* McGraw Hill, New York, N.Y., 1966.

CARROLL, JOHN M. *Careers and Opportunities in Computer Science,* E. P. Dutton & Co., New York, N.Y., 1967.

COOK, JOSEPH J. *The Electronic Brain: How It Works,* G. P. Putnam's Sons, New York, N.Y., 1969.

HARVILL, JOHN B. *Basic FORTRAN Programming,* Prentice-Hall, Englewood Cliffs, N.J., 1968.

KINSLER, DORIS and STEPHEN. *Computers: Machines with a Memory,* Hawthorn Books, New York, N.Y., 1968.

KOHN, BERNICE. *Computers at Your Service,* Prentice-Hall, Englewood Cliffs, N.J., 1962.

LYSEGARD, ANNA. *Introduction to COBOL,* Oxford University Press, New York, N.Y., 1968.

NIKOLAIEFF, GEORGE A., ed. *Computers and Society,* H. W. Wilson Co., New York, N.Y., 1970.

PIPER, ROGER. *The Story of Computers,* Harcourt Brace Jovanovich, New York, N.Y., 1964.

VON NEUMANN, JOHN. *The Computer and the Brain,* Yale University Press, New Haven, Conn., 1958.

# Index

179